Chinese
Massage
Manual

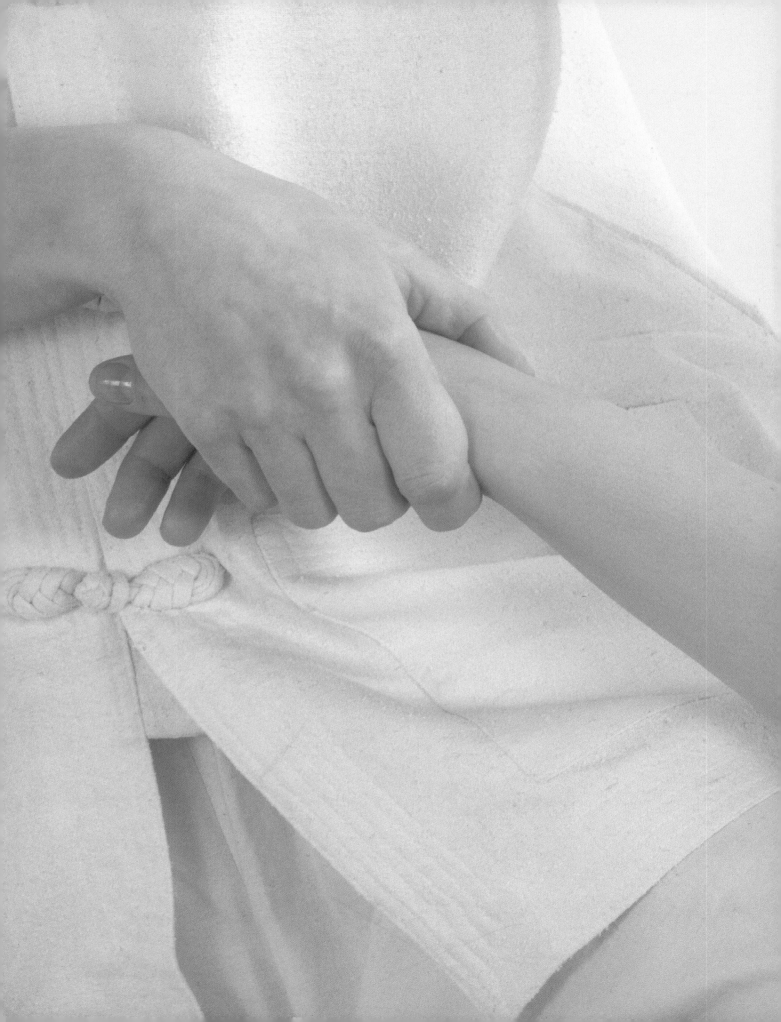

Chinese Massage Manual

A comprehensive, step-by-step guide to the healing art of Tui Na

Sarah Pritchard

Foreword by Li He

Photography by Sue Atkinson

PIATKUS

Dedicated to the memory of Claudia Cran

First published in 1999 by Judy Piatkus (Publishers) Ltd of
5 Windmill Street, London W1P 1HF

A catalogue record for this book is available from the British Library

ISBN 0-7499-2053-X

AN EDDISON•SADD EDITION
Edited, designed and produced by
Eddison Sadd Editions Limited
St Chad's House
148 King's Cross Road
London WC1X 9DH

Phototypeset in Hiroshige and MGillSans using QuarkXPress on Apple Macintosh
Origination by Pixel Graphics, Singapore
Printed by Shenzhen Donnelley, Bright Sun, China

Contents

Foreword

Tui Na – Chinese Medical Massage – is an important component in Traditional Chinese Medicine. In China, it shares the same eminence as acupuncture, herbal medicine and other Chinese medical treatments. Tui Na is, in fact, one of the earliest treatment methods used by humankind in primeval Chinese society. It has since undergone several thousand years of clinical development and practice, resulting in a discipline that is unique and comprehensive, and that aligns its theory perfectly with its practise.

The subject of Tui Na has been well documented throughout its 5,000 years of Chinese history. The classic writings on Chinese medicine, such as *Nei Jing*, written over 2,000 years ago, contain detailed descriptions of the concept, theory and application of Tui Na. However, when lecturing at the London School of Chinese Clinical Massage Therapy a few years ago, I was unable to find any suitable material written in English to recommend to my pupils.

Sarah Pritchard's book changes all this, offering the Tui Na student an alternative to the traditional Chinese textbook. Its concise explanation of the concept, its clear documentation of the theory and its accurate description of the technique all contribute to a easy-to-follow and practical guide, which is essential to anyone who is interested in Chinese massage. Reading between the lines, it will become evident to you that no time and effort, however minute, was spared in its construction – hard work that should be duly admired and appreciated indeed.

Practising and lecturing in the United Kingdom has given me the privilege of working with experts of other therapeutic disciplines. While it must be acknowledged that each of these methods undoubtedly has its own strength, it must also be noted that in many cases Tui Na produces inimitable results. Similar to other methods of Chinese medicine, such as acupuncture and herbal medicine, already practised in a foreign context, the popularization of Tui Na in the West will bring innumerable benefits, both in its capacity as a complementary treatment and as a rewarding activity for the practitioner. So much more than a manual, this book stimulates this cultural exchange between East and West, encouraging an integration of our medical systems for the future.

Li He holds an Advanced Diploma from the Academy of Chinese Medicine, Beijing, majoring in acupuncture and Tui Na. Dr Li now runs a busy clinic in London.

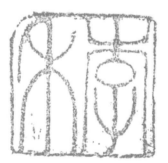

Dr H. Li, 1999

Introduction

Tui Na is one of the four main branches of traditional Chinese medicine; its sister therapies are Chinese herbal medicine, acupuncture and Qi Gong. Tui Na is relatively new to the West but its roots in China are ancient. Archaeological studies have dated it back to around 2700 BC, making it the forefather of all forms of massage and body work that exist today, from shiatsu to osteopathy. Throughout its history, Tui Na has been developed, refined and systemized by doctors in the colleges and hospitals of traditional Chinese medicine all over China. Tui Na is a very popular form of treatment with the people in China and it is not at all unusual to see people queuing up in long lines outside the hospitals waiting for the Tui Na department to open. It is also the first choice of treatment for infants and children.

Tui Na differs from other forms of massage in that it is used to treat specific illnesses of an internal nature as well as musculoskeletal ailments. The Tui Na practitioner must have a thorough understanding of the rationale of traditional Chinese medicine in order to make a diagnosis according to its principles. This is essential before treatment can begin. The treatment itself involves the use of a wide range of specific manual techniques, all of which have particular effects and areas of influence.

Many people in the West have been drawn to and helped by Chinese herbal medicine and acupuncture. Now Tui Na is beginning to spread throughout the West and its popularity is growing daily as people begin to reap the benefits of this therapy as they have done in China for thousands of years.

This book aims to provide an overall introduction to the various aspects of Tui Na. It is laid out in three parts. Part one is an introduction to the building blocks of the theory of traditional Chinese medicine. Part two gives practical user-friendly instruction on how to apply twenty commonly used Tui Na techniques plus Qi Gong exercises for building up general health, strength and stamina. Part three puts the two together, providing simple treatments for common ailments, such as headaches and period pains. Everything is laid out as simply and clearly as possible, making the information and instructions accessible to anyone who is interested – from the patient and lay practitioner to the budding Tui Na student and practitioners of related therapies.

One thing I have learned about Chinese medicine is that there is always more to learn and, in practice, it is the people coming for treatment who become our greatest teachers. Having gained some insights into the rationale of traditional Chinese medicine, the Tui Na techniques will be more meaningful and you will be able to make sense of their individual effects. With a little work and patience, the theory and techniques will all come together and you will be able to put your knowledge into practice with your friends and family.

Sarah Pritchard, 1999

The history of Tui Na

The history of Tui Na is a long one. Evidence from archaeological digs suggests that it was first practised over 3,000 years ago. Ancient oracle bones were discovered upon which there are inscriptions that refer to a female shaman known as a Bi who healed people with massage manipulations.

In the late Zhou dynasty (700–481 BC), texts on the development of Chinese medicine refer to massage or 'An Wu', as it was called. There is mention of a Dr Bian Que working with a combination of massage and acupuncture simultaneously.

The most famous ancient text on Chinese medicine is 'Huang Di Nei Jing' or 'Classic of Internal Medicine of the Yellow Emperor', which was completed between the first century BC and the first century AD. It includes records of the use of massage as medicine and refers to twelve massage techniques and how they should be used in the treatment of certain diseases.

The evolution of a medical system

Massage continued to develop along with the rest of Chinese medicine. Then, during the Sui (AD 581–618) and Tang (AD 618–906) dynasties, massage therapy really started to flourish. A department of massage therapy was founded within the Office of Imperial Physicians and the practice and teaching of Chinese massage therapy continued to blossom. Dr Sun Si Miao introduced a further ten massage techniques and systemized the treatment of childhood diseases using massage therapy.

During this period in history a text was written known as 'Six Classics in the Tang Dynasty', listing the range of diseases treatable with massage therapy. Through this, massage therapy took its place as a medical treatment in its own right. From this point it began to spread to other countries, such as Korea, Vietnam, Japan and Islam.

In the Song dynasty (AD 960–1279) and the Yuan dynasty (AD 1280–1368), an intensive analysis of Chinese massage techniques was undertaken and the therapy was further refined. It became the major form of treatment in the bone-setting and paediatric departments at the Institute of Imperial Physicians.

The Ming dynasty (AD 1368–1644) saw the next great flourishing of massage therapy. It was during this time that it took the name Tui Na. Many texts were written during this period, particularly on paediatric Tui Na, which had become hugely popular. Tui Na specialists from all over China met to discuss diagnosis, techniques and treatments. During the Qing dynasty (AD 1644–1912), Tui Na continued to develop and thrive in both imperial and public domains.

Western medicine versus Chinese medicine

In the early part of the twentieth century, traditional Chinese medicine began to suffer greatly. This was due to competition from the mainly symptomatic treatments of Western medicine now available. There was, in fact, a time when it looked like traditional Chinese medicine would die out completely. Between 1912–48, during the rule of Guo Min Dang, doctors trained in Western medicine returned to China from Japan and recommended that traditional Chinese medicine be banned. Fortunately, this was rejected at the National Medical Assembly in Shanghai on 17 March 1929, thanks to massive lobbying. This day is remembered each year and celebrated as Chinese Doctors' Day.

Mao Ze Dong was also against traditional Chinese medicine until the Long March of 1934–35. There were no drugs, anaesthetics or surgery available, and doctors of traditional Chinese medicine came to the rescue, achieving amazing results with vast numbers of wounded and sick soldiers.

From this time on, traditional Chinese medicine (TCM) had its feet planted firmly on the ground of modern medicine and, under the People's Republic of China established in 1948, all the departments of TCM were nurtured and encouraged to grow. In 1956, the first official training course in Tui Na was opened in Shanghai; other hospitals followed suit, opening their own Tui Na departments. By 1974, Tui Na training departments had been set up all over China. By 1978, whole hospitals were devoted to the practice of TCM and all other hospitals held within them special TCM departments. International training centres for TCM were established in Beijing, Nanjing and Shanghai. In 1987, the Chinese National Tui Na Association was established and holds regular meetings for Tui Na doctors to share their clinical experience and offer papers on their work.

The future of Tui Na

Traditional Chinese medicine has become increasingly popular in the West over the last twenty years as a growing number of individuals seek alternatives to conventional drugs. More and more research into the effects of acupuncture, Chinese herbs, Tui Na and Qi Gong is already taking place, and the minds of Western doctors are beginning to open as their patients consistently report back the curative effects of traditional Chinese treatments. As we move further into the twenty-first century, I believe we will see an integration of TCM and other forms of complementary medicine with Western medicine. This would provide people with a health system that takes the best aspects from all forms of medicine, resulting in a greater choice of treatments and minimizing side effects and costs. As doctors and practitioners come to work together, the overall health and well-being of the public at large can only benefit.

Tui Na in practice
Sarah Pritchard working on a patient at the Second Teaching Hospital of Nanjing University of Traditional Chinese Medicine in 1994.

The Theory

Chinese massage is inseparable from theory. It is as essential for a Tui Na practitioner to have a clear understanding of the rationale of Chinese medicine as it is for an acupuncturist or a practitioner of Chinese herbal medicine. To learn the massage techniques alone would be like teaching an acupuncturist to insert a needle and no more. To practise Tui Na, you need to *understand* what you are doing.

Part one will introduce you to the main building blocks of the theory of traditional Chinese medicine. It is not the purpose of this book to provide a detailed account of all aspects of theory, but rather to give you a taste for it. If this system of medicine fascinates and captures you as much as it did me, I recommend that you add one or two of the books listed at the back of the book to your collection.

As you read through this book, you will notice that the language of Chinese medicine is quite different from that of Western medicine. Many of the terms used to describe disease and disharmony – such as 'spleen Qi deficiency' or 'wind-heat invading the lungs' – may be quite unfamiliar to you. Don't be put off by these words, and steer clear of comparing Chinese medicine with any knowledge you have of Western medicine, as this can lead to much confusion. Chinese medicine is an energetic rather than a mechanistic form of medicine, so the language used is descriptive of what is happening energetically within a human being. If energy is not moving freely somewhere in the body, it is referred to as 'stagnating'. If this is the case, you – as the practitioner – must 'restore the smooth flow of energy' or 'disperse stagnant energy'. If someone has 'damp' within them, then the 'damp' must be 'drained' or 'resolved'; likewise, if energy is deficient, it must be 'strengthened' or 'tonified'. These everyday words may not be the way you expect medicine to be described, but they are the building blocks of Chinese medicine. So, keep an open mind, use your imagination and try to visualize what the language is describing.

Yin Yang Theory

The Chinese character for Yin means 'the shady side of a hill'.

The Chinese character for Yang means 'the sunny side of a hill'.

Tao (pronounced 'Dao') means 'the way of right action', and Taoist thought understands that a part can only be really understood in relation to the whole. Yin Yang theory is the core root of traditional Chinese medicine, providing an all-encompassing logic to aid the explanation of all relationships, patterns and change in the vast macrocosm of the universe – and therefore the mirrored microcosm of the human being.

The labels of Yin and Yang help us describe how one thing functions in relation to another. Nothing exists in the universe in isolation, but only in relation to all other things. The five sentences below describe Yin and Yang.

Yin and Yang are relative opposites

All that exists can be described as being either Yin or Yang by nature in relation to something else. For example, day is Yang in relation to night, which is Yin. Physical activity is Yang in relation to rest, which is Yin. The health of the entire universe, and therefore the health of human beings, relies on the continuous shifting cyclical movements of these relative opposites.

Yin and Yang are infinitely divisible

Temperature can be divided into cold (Yin) and hot (Yang) but cold could further be divided into icy cold (Yin) and moderately cold (Yang). In the human body the front is Yin in relation to the back, which is Yang, but we could divide the front, for example, so that the abdomen is Yin in relation to the chest, which becomes relatively Yang.

Yin and Yang are interdependent

Yin cannot exist without Yang and vice versa; each totally depends on the other. There cannot be light without dark, contraction without expansion, above without below. Just as the earth needs rainfall (Yin) and dryness (Yang) to survive, a mutually balanced relationship between Yin and Yang is vital in the body.

Yin and Yang consume and support one another

The balance between Yin and Yang is not a fixed state but a constant flux achieved by the dynamic movement and shifting levels of the two forces. Night consumes day; summer consumes winter. If Yin and Yang become out of balance, then disharmony can occur. If one becomes very weak, it cannot support the other; or, if one becomes excessive, it may over-consume the other.

Yin and Yang transform into each other

Yin and Yang are constantly transforming into each other: inhalation is followed by exhalation, activity is followed by rest. This transformation can be witnessed in the human body. During an acute feverish disease, when the fever peaks the pulse is rapid and full (Yang), then all of a sudden the individual becomes cold and the pulse thin (Yin). In this situation, Yang has reached its extreme; it can go no further and transforms into Yin.

'The Tao is the one

From the one come Yin and Yang

From these two, creative Qi

From Qi, ten thousand things

The forms of all creation' (Tao 42)

Yin		Yang
Water		Fire
Moon		Sun
Dark		Bright
Heavy		Light
Descending		Ascending
Damp		Dry
Cold		Hot
Below		Above
Inside		Outside
Slow		Fast
Matter		Energy
Rest		Activity
Contraction		Expansion

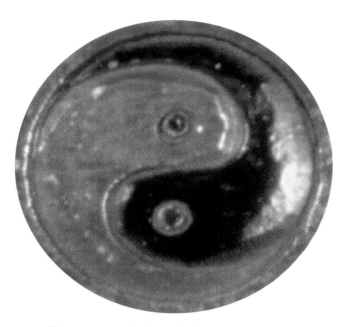

The symbol of Yin and Yang
This dynamic symbol helps us to grasp how opposites can be in a constant state of flux and mutual support. Here it is surrounded by examples of relative opposites.

The importance of balance

All diseases and disharmonies are due to an imbalance of Yin and Yang energies within a human being, and all diseases can be defined as either Yin or Yang. If Yang becomes deficient, an individual will begin to manifest symptoms associated with Yin (such as weakness and coldness) as the Yin energy appears to be dominant. If, on the other hand, Yin becomes deficient, then Yang symptoms will manifest (such as insomnia and feeling hot). If Yang or Yin energies become excessive, they will have a detrimental effect on the other. Excessive heat (Yang), for example, will burn up body fluids (Yin). And too much dampness (Yin) will put out the fire (Yang).

The concept of Yin and Yang is simple and profound. However, it is so all encompassing that it can escape our reach. Therefore, as traditional Chinese medicine developed, the theory of the eight guiding principles was formed (see pages 26–9) which subdivides Yin and Yang into more usable guidance for the practitioner of traditional Chinese medicine.

Classifying symptoms

All symptoms can be divided into Yin or Yang. If Yin becomes deficient, a person will experience symptoms associated with Yang, and vice versa.

Yin	Yang
Chronic disease	Acute disease
Slow onset of symptoms	Sudden onset of symptoms
Pale complexion	Flushed complexion
Cold limbs and body	Hot limbs and body
Likes heat	Likes cold
Dislikes cold	Dislikes heat
Tiredness	Restlessness
Sleepiness	Insomnia
Quiet and still	Loud and hyperactive
Slow, deep, weak pulse	Rapid, full, superficial pulse

Five Elements Theory

The Chinese character for 'five' is Wu.

The Chinese character for 'element' is Xing, which also means process, movement or phase.

Five elements theory and Yin Yang theory form the basic building blocks of traditional Chinese medical theory. Five elements theory – Wu Xing, in Chinese – developed much later than that of Yin Yang. The first documentation on the subject dates from around 476–221BC. From this time, throughout Chinese history, the five elements theory has ebbed and flowed in its popularity and has been applied not only to medicine but also to other aspects of society such as politics and music.

The five elements are represented as wood, fire, earth, metal and water. All things in the universe, such as seasons, climates, emotions and internal organs, correspond to one of these five natural qualities. As with Yin and Yang, the five elements are constantly pursuing harmonious relationships with each other. They rely on each other for their existence and management. If one element becomes too weak or too dominant, then all the others will also be affected.

Major correspondences of the five elements

	Wood	Fire	Earth	Metal	Water
Climate	Wind	Heat	Dampness	Dryness	Cold
Season	Spring	Summer	Late summer	Autumn	Winter
Direction	East	South	Centre	West	North
Number	8	7	5	9	6
Planet	Jupiter	Mars	Saturn	Venus	Mercury
Movement	Outward expansion	Upward	Neutral	Inward contraction	Downward
Colour	Blue-green	Red	Yellow	White	Black
Taste	Sour	Bitter	Sweet	Pungent	Salty
Sound	Shouting	Laughing	Singing	Crying	Groaning
Smell	Rancid	Scorched	Fragrant	Rotten	Putrid
Emotion	Anger	Joy	Worry/pensiveness	Grief/sadness	Fear
Yin organ	Liver	Heart	Spleen	Lungs	Kidneys
Yang organ	Gall bladder	Small intestine	Stomach	Large intestine	Bladder
Sense organ	Eyes	Tongue	Mouth	Nose	Ears
Tissues	Tendons	Blood vessels	Muscles	Skin	Bones
Stage of development	Birth	Growth	Transformation	Harvest	Storage

The cycles of the five elements

In the vast macrocosm of our universe and its mirrored microcosm of the human being, the five elements are constantly interacting. Each element generates or 'gives birth to' another element. The diagram below illustrates this birthing, or generating, cycle.

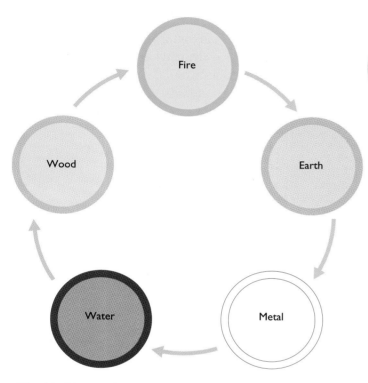

The birthing cycle
Wood gives birth to fire, fire gives birth to earth, earth gives birth to metal, metal gives birth to water and water gives birth to wood.

The element that gives birth is called the mother and the element that is born is called the child. For example, earth is the mother of metal and the child of fire. Each element is the mother of the next element in the birthing cycle and the child of the previous element.

The five elements also control each other *(see diagram above, right)*. The combination of the birthing and controlling cycles provides harmony and balance to the five elements. The cycles are interconnected: water controls fire, but fire gives birth to earth and so on.

If disharmony occurs within the elements' relationships, it is possible for one element to over-control another or to 'insult' another. The insulting cycle is the controlling cycle in reverse. For example, earth insults wood and fire insults water.

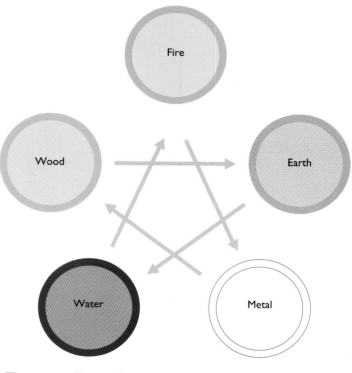

The controlling cycle
Wood controls earth and is controlled by metal. Earth controls water and is controlled by wood. Water controls fire and is controlled by earth. Fire controls metal and is controlled by water. Metal controls wood and is controlled by fire.

Relating the cycles to the organs

You will notice from the table of correspondences *(opposite)* that each of the internal organs is associated with an element: the liver and gall bladder correspond to wood, the spleen and stomach to earth, and the kidneys and bladder to water. We have said that each element is born from, gives birth to and controls another element, and the same is true of the organs. The heart is the mother of the spleen and the child of the liver; the spleen is the mother of the lungs and the child of the heart.

The organs are kept in balance through the controlling cycle. The liver controls the spleen; the heart controls the lungs; the spleen controls the kidneys; the lungs control the liver and the kidneys control the heart. Saying that one organ controls another does not mean that one organ forcibly restrains or represses another – this would be regarded as over-controlling and as a sign of disharmony. In good health, the controlling cycle of

15

Case history

Name Natasha

Age 32 years

Symptoms

This young woman came to see me, having recently experienced the death of her mother. Shortly after the funeral she caught a cold which quickly developed into bronchitis. She has a pale, white complexion and says, 'I just keep bursting into tears'. She also complains of dry skin which has become worse over the past month since her mother's death.

Diagnosis

These symptoms point clearly to disharmony of the metal element which is associated with the lungs. Grief and sadness dissolve Qi *(see page 23)* and weaken the lungs. In this case, the lungs' defensive Qi, which protects the body from invasions of exterior pathogens, has become weak from the huge sadness Natasha is feeling. Therefore she is susceptible and develops a cold. Then, as her resistance is low, this moves deeper into the lungs to become bronchitis. Her white complexion, dry skin and frequent crying are all linked to a deficiency of the metal element.

Treatment principle

As a practitioner, you could use stimulation of points *(see 58 Key Points, pages 48–53)* to strengthen metal (the lungs) and strengthen the element which gives birth to metal – which is earth (the spleen) – so that earth can help by giving extra nourishment to its child.

the organs means that each organ supports and aids another. For example, the heart supports and aids the lungs, while the lungs support and aid the liver. The diagram below illustrates the careful balance of these relationships.

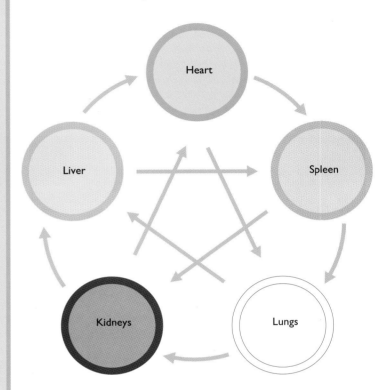

The birthing and controlling cycles for the organs
The heart is the mother of the spleen and the child of the liver; the spleen is the mother of the lungs and the child of the heart, and so on. The liver controls the spleen; the heart controls the lungs; the spleen controls the kidneys; the lungs control the liver and the kidneys control the heart.

Applying the theory of the five elements

The theory of the five elements offers the practitioner a useful guideline to aid diagnosis. If one of the elements is out of balance in an individual, they may show signs and symptoms associated with that element *(as shown in the table of correspondences on page 14)*. Natasha's case history *(left)* clearly illustrates the point.

Vital Substances

 Qi

 Blood

 Jing (essence)

 *Jin Ye (body fluids)*

The four vital substances are: Qi (pronounced 'chee'), blood, essence and body fluids. In Chinese medicine it is believed that these substances form and maintain the human body and mind. The internal organs, meridians, tissues, bones and sense organs are dependent on these vital substances for the energy, nourishment and lubrication they require to perform their various functions. At the same time, the vital substances are dependent on the internal organs, meridians, tissues, and so on, for their production, storage and metabolism.

Qi is the basis of all the other vital substances, which are basically Qi in various forms, ranging from the material to the non-material. For the Tui Na practitioner, the most important substances are Qi and blood – keep these in mind when you are treating a patient.

Qi

The Chinese character for Qi is made up of two parts: the first part means vapour or steam, and the second part means rice. This implies that Qi is both solid matter, like rice, yet rarefied and non-material, like vapour. It is therefore, by nature, both Yin and Yang. There are many translations of the word Qi from Mandarin into English, such as 'energy', 'life force', 'vital force', 'moving power', but none truly captures the nature of Qi.

We could say that Qi is everything that exists. All phenomena, all change, all the myriad forms in the universe are made of Qi and defined by their Qi. Qi is matter at the point of becoming energy and energy at the point of becoming matter. In the human body, Qi is constantly changing and takes on different roles depending on what it needs to do in the body and where. The tables overleaf indicate the different forms of Qi in the body, their functions, and what can go wrong with them.

Qi produces the human body

just as water becomes ice.

As water freezes into ice, so Qi

coagulates to form the human body.

When a person dies, he or she

becomes spirit again.

It is called spirit just as melted ice

changes its name to water.

WANG CHONG (AD 27–97)

17

Different forms of Qi

Yuan Qi	*Original or source Qi* This is made up from both kidney essence (Jing) and the Qi formed from food and air. Yuan Qi is the foundation for all the other types of Qi in the body.
Zang Fu Qi	*Organ Qi* This is Yuan Qi at work as the functions of the internal organs.
Jingluo Qi	*Meridian Qi* This is Yuan Qi moving through the meridian system, communicating with the whole body. When a point is stimulated it is this Qi that is felt as a strong sensation at the point or along the meridian.
Gu Qi	*Food Qi* This is the first refinement of digested food from the spleen.
Zhen Qi	*Upright or correct Qi* This is a further refinement of digested food and air which has two aspects: Ying Qi and Wei Qi.
Ying Qi	*Nutritive Qi* This forms blood and moves with it through the vessels, nourishing the organs and limbs.
Wei Qi	*Defensive Qi* This moves on the exterior of the body outside the vessels, regulating the skin and pores and protecting the body from invasions of external pathogenic factors, such as wind or cold *(see page 24–25)*. It also warms the organs.
Zong Qi	*Gathering Qi* Gathers in the chest and influences the lungs and heart.

Functions of Qi

Activates	Qi creates change and movement and drives the metabolism.
Warms	Qi creates heat throughout the body.
Raises	Qi supports the internal organs, so they do not prolapse, and ascends clear Yang energy.
Defends	As Wei Qi it fights external pathogenic factors. As Zhen Qi it fights internal pathogenic factors.
Transforms	Qi transforms food, drink and air into blood and body fluids; and transforms body fluids into sweat and urine.
Contains	Qi holds blood within the vessels and fluids within their correct boundaries.

What can go wrong with Qi

Deficient Qi	If Qi becomes insufficient, it cannot perform its functions. If spleen Qi is deficient, its function of transforming and transporting food and fluids suffers, leading to disease.
Stagnant Qi	The flow of Qi through the body becomes impaired. Qi can stagnate in the meridians, causing musculoskeletal problems, or in internal organs. Stagnant liver Qi may lead to abdominal pain. Qi moves the blood, so Qi stagnation affects blood movement.
Collapsed Qi	When Qi becomes very weak it may not be able to perform its function of raising, which keeps internal organs in place. Qi collapses or falls, and prolapses can occur, such as piles.
Rebellious Qi	Qi moves in the opposite direction to its normal flow. Stomach Qi should descend; if it rebels upwards it can cause nausea and vomiting. Spleen Qi should ascend; if it rebels downwards it can cause diarrhoea.

Blood

血 Blood is formed by the transformation of food. The stomach 'rots and ripens' food, then the spleen transforms it into Gu Qi (Food Qi) and transports this up to the lungs. It becomes red blood through the transformative influence of Ying Qi (nutritive Qi) and the lungs.

Blood flows through blood vessels and meridians under the governance of the heart, nourishing the whole body. It is stored in the liver when the body is at rest and regulated by the liver when the body is in motion. It is contained or held within the vessels by the management of the spleen.

Qi and blood are interdependent. In Chinese medicine it is said that 'Qi is the commander of blood' – blood is produced, held within its boundaries, stored, regulated and circulated by Qi. It is also said that 'blood is the mother of Qi' – blood gives nourishment to sustain Qi in the body. In Chinese medicine there are three disorders of blood.

Blood deficiency
This could give rise to symptoms such as dizziness, tiredness, palpitations, blurred vision, dryness, stiff limbs, numbness, cramp and pale-coloured face, lips and nails.

Blood stasis
This could give rise to symptoms such as a stabbing pain in a fixed location, fixed lumps, bleeding and purple-coloured lips, tongue and general complexion.

Blood heat
This could give rise to symptoms such as bleeding bright-red blood, restlessness, skin eruptions, delirium and even coma.

Essence – Jing

津 Jing, or Essence, is a thick, slow-moving, refined substance which has different aspects. Pre-heaven – or congenital – Jing is inherited from our parents. It cannot be increased; what we are born with is all we get. However, it can be preserved through spiritual practices, such as meditation.

Post-heaven – or acquired – Jing, on the other hand is formed by the body from food and air. It is constantly being replenished and supports the pre-heaven Jing.

Jing Qi, or the Essence, comes from both pre- and post-heaven Jing. It is stored in the kidneys and travels throughout the body maintaining the internal organs. Only when it is plentiful in the organs can it be stored in the kidneys.

Jing has five functions:

- It controls growth, reproduction and development.
- It produces marrow.
- It resists external pathogens.
- It produces blood.
- It is the source of kidney Qi.

Disorders of Jing can be caused by a number of problems. These include congenital problems, cerebral dysfunction, blood deficiency, susceptibility to disease, and sexual, back, knee and ear problems.

Body fluids – Jin Ye

液 In Chinese medicine, the body fluids are called Jin Ye. They have the functions of nourishing and moistening the blood, internal organs, skin, sense organs, muscles, marrow and hair. There are two different types of body fluids: the Jin – clear, thin fluids – and the Ye – thick, turbid fluids. These two forms can transform one into the other.

The stomach is the origin of body fluids. The spleen transforms and transports them. The lungs disperse and descend them. The kidneys send the clear fluids upwards and the thick, turbid fluids downwards. The small intestine separates the pure fluids from the impure fluids. The triple burner distributes them throughout the body. Body fluids can become deficient or they can stagnate.

Body fluid deficiency
This can cause symptoms such as constipation, stiffness, emaciation, cramp and dry mouth, eyes, nose, skin, hair and lips.

Body fluid stagnation
This can lead to symptoms such as oedema, swelling, stuffy chest and lack of sweating.

Internal Organs

The Chinese character for Zang

The Chinese character for Fu

Western medicine initially defines an organ in terms of its physical anatomy *(see anatomical illustration, page 46)*. In Chinese medicine, on the other hand, the internal organs – or Zang Fu – are perceived in terms of their functions, the relationships they have with each other and their relationships with the vital substances, sense organs, tissues, emotions, mental functions, aspects of the soul and environmental factors.

The theory of the internal organs gives a clear picture of the holistic approach of Chinese medicine. Everything is seen as an integrated whole. By nature, this is an *energetic* rather than *mechanistic* medicine. Therefore, organs such as the triple burner, which has no anatomical structure, can be recognized.

The organs are divided into Yin and Yang. There are five Zang-Yin organs: the heart, lungs, liver, spleen, kidneys. There is also the pericardium, but it is regarded as part of the heart. There are six Fu-Yang organs: the small intestine, large intestine, stomach, gall bladder, bladder and triple burner. The Yin organs are regarded as the most important; they store the pure vital substances. The Yang organs digest, transform, move, receive and excrete.

The table *(right)* describes each of the Zang-Yin organs, indicating the organ's functions and various relationships.

Functions and relationships of internal organs

Heart	Liver
Governs blood and blood vessels Regulates the flow of blood.	**Stores blood** Regulates blood volume and menstruation. Blood flows back to liver when the body is at rest.
Houses the mind Mental activity, emotions, memory, consciousness, thinking, sleep.	**Regulates the flow of Qi** Ensures Qi moves smoothly throughout whole of body in all directions.
Manifests in the complexion The energetic state of the heart shows in the colour of the complexion.	**Manifests in the nails** Colour, moisture, texture etc.
Controls sweat If heart Qi is deficient it can lead to spontaneous sweating.	**Controls the sinews** Disharmony of liver could lead to cramp, spasm, tremors, contracted muscles/tendons.
Opens into the tongue Disharmony of heart can lead to spleen problems, ulceration, inflammation of tongue.	**Opens into the eyes** Vision, visual disturbances etc.
Relates to the emotion joy	**Relates to the emotion anger** Gives mental ability of planning our lives and creative drive.
Related Yang organ is the small intestine	**Related Yang organ is the gall bladder**
Dislikes heat	**Dislikes wind**

Lungs

Govern Qi and respiration
Inhalation and exhalation of air and Qi. Help create Qi.

Descend and disperse Qi
Spread defensive Qi between skin and muscles to protect body. Descend Qi to kidneys.

Regulate water passages
Disperse fluids to skin and direct fluids downwards to bladder.

Manifest in the skin and hair
Moisture, lustre, etc.

Control channels and vessels
Circulation of Qi and blood in blood vessels and meridians.

Open into the nose
Sense of smell, blocked nose, etc.

Relate to the emotions of sadness and grief
Govern strength of voice

Related Yang organ is the large intestine

Dislike cold

Spleen

Governs transformation and transportation
Transforms food and drink into Qi and blood.

Controls blood
Holds blood in the vessels.

Raises Qi
Keeps organs in their correct place.

Manifests in the lips
Moisture, colour, texture, etc.

Controls muscles
Spleen disharmony could lead to weak muscles.

Opens into the mouth
Sense of taste.

Relates to thought
Influences studying, focusing, memorizing and concentrating.

Related Yang organ is the stomach

Dislikes dampness

Kidneys

Govern growth, birth, reproduction and development
Produce marrow. Essence produces marrow, which makes spinal cord and fills the brain. Govern bones. Marrow is basis for bones and bone marrow.

Store Essence (Jing)
Pre-heaven and post-heaven.

Receive Qi from the lungs
Hold Qi down to prevent congestion in chest.

Manifest in the hair
Growth, health, shine. Weak kidneys can lead to baldness.

Control water
The flow of body fluids in the lower burner. Control the lower orifices: anus, urethra, genitals.

Open into the ears
Hearing.

Relate to the emotion fear
House will-power.

Related Yang organ is the bladder

Dislike dryness

Pericardium

The protector of the heart. In practice it is not separate to the heart: its only separate function is to protect the heart from external pathogenic factors. Its related Yang organ is the triple burner.

The Triple Burner

The triple burner or San Jiao has no structure. The triple burner represents a passageway for body fluids and controls the overall movement of fluids in the entire body. It is an energetic container for the internal organs and has three aspects:

1 The upper burner which represents the chest and houses the heart and lungs is seen like a mist circulating fine fluids over the skin and all around the body.

2 The middle burner encompasses the area between the diaphragm and the navel, housing the stomach and spleen. It is seen like a maceration chamber, the place where food and drink are broken down, 'rotted and ripened'.

3 The lower burner is below the navel and houses the liver, kidneys, bladder, intestines and uterus and is seen like a drainage system – separating fluids and excreting waste.

Causes of Disease

In Chinese medicine, disease is regarded as an expression of some kind of disharmony occurring within an person's energetic system. Finding the cause of a pattern of disharmony is of vital importance to the practitioner, as part of his or her work is about guiding the patients towards an awareness of the cause of their problem and providing advice, encouragement and support regarding changes the patient may need to make in their lives in order to restore harmony and balance and to help prevent further disharmony from occurring. The changes required are often multifold.

The causes of disease fall into three categories, covered over the next few pages: internal causes, external causes and miscellaneous causes.

Internal causes – emotions

Joy

Worry

Anger

Fear

Sadness

Shock

Grief

In Chinese medicine, the physical body is inseparable from the mind and emotions, and the internal organs are at the root of this integration. The Qi of the five Yin organs produces emotions and, in turn, the Yin organs are affected by emotions. When in balance, emotion provides us with the motivation to drive our bodies and live our lives. An emotion only becomes a cause of disease if it is very intense or felt over an extended period of time, especially if it is repressed and given no channel of expression. Just as emotions can cause disharmony of the internal organs, so disharmony can cause emotions. For example, an individual with a lung disharmony may feel tearful and sad.

There are seven emotions in Chinese medicine, listed below. Each affects one or more organs and has a particular influence on Qi. In general, if emotions are out of balance, they cause Qi stagnation and, over time, create internal heat and fire which can damage, primarily, the liver, heart, lungs or kidneys.

Joy

Joy slows Qi down and affects the heart. Joy refers to a state of over-excitement or constant mental stimulation which can, over time, create patterns of disharmony, like heart Yin deficiency or heart fire.

Anger

Anger makes Qi rise and affects the liver. Anger also refers to feelings like resentment, bitterness, frustration, irritability, rage. If, for example, a person is frustrated

Emotions and their effects on the body			Symptoms
Joy	Slows Qi Affects heart	Heart Yin deficiency Heart fire	Insomnia, palpitations, poor memory Fever, agitation, mental imbalance, delirium
Anger	Raises Qi Affects liver	Liver Yang rising/fire blazing Liver Qi stagnation	Headaches, dizziness, tinnitus Abdominal pain, menstrual pain, feeling a lump in the throat, depression, lack of confidence
Sadness/grief	Dissolve Qi Affect lungs	Lung Qi deficiency	Tiredness, breathlessness, depression
Pensiveness	Knots Qi Affects spleen	Spleen Qi deficiency	Low appetite, loose stools, tiredness
Fear	Descends Qi Affects kidneys	Kidney Yin deficiency	Night sweats, dry mouth and throat, a feeling of heat
Shock	Scatters Qi Affects kidneys and heart	Sudden depletion of heart and kidney Qi	Palpitations, insomnia, breathlessness, night sweats, dizziness

and resentful and represses these feelings, they can build up internally and, over time, cause symptoms like abdominal pain and lack of confidence.

Sadness and grief

Sadness and grief dissolve Qi and affect the lungs. In time the lungs are weakened by these emotions. The heart is also affected due to its close relationship with the lungs in the upper burner.

Pensiveness

Pensiveness and worry knot Qi and affect, primarily, the spleen, but also the lungs. Over-thinking, excessive studying and fretting can weaken the spleen.

Fear

Fear makes Qi descend and affects the kidneys. It can cause patterns of disharmony like kidney Yin deficiency.

Shock

Shock scatters Qi and affects both the kidneys and the heart. Shock or extreme fear causes a sudden depletion of heart and kidney Qi.

Case history

Name David

Age 44 years

Symptoms
David was suffering with very bad migraine headaches.

Diagnosis
Liver Yang rising caused by repression of feelings over a long period of time, plus inappropriate diet.

Treatment
David needed to make changes in his diet, cutting out foods like chocolate and coffee, and to make time in his daily routine for relaxation. He also needed to find ways of expressing his feelings rather than keeping them to himself. With David's determination and openness the frequency of the migraines was greatly reduced.

23

External causes – climatic conditions

Wind

Cold

Damp

Summer heat

Dryness

Fire

can become depleted. The first line of defence is the Wei Qi, or defensive Qi. If this is deficient, it becomes possible for external climatic factors to invade the body via the surface, through the skin, mouth, nose and the most external and vulnerable organ, the lungs.

Depending on the strength of the pathogenic factor and the relative weakness of the Qi, they can penetrate deeper into the body, into the muscles, bones and joints and the meridians. Eventually, they can penetrate the internal organs; this is most likely to occur if a person already has a pattern of disharmony within a particular organ. Opposite is a table listing the characteristics, typical symptoms and examples of diseases associated with each of the external pathogenic factors.

There are many ways external climatic conditions can affect the body. One of the most obvious is when you go out for a walk on a windy day without adequate clothing; the next day you may have symptoms of sneezing, running nose, upper-body aches and headache. These indicate an invasion of wind cold. Likewise, sleeping next to an open window is often the cause of wryneck: waking up with an acutely stiff and painful neck. Walking around with bare feet on damp grass can lead to an invasion of damp, which can rise through the leg meridians settling in the joints and leading to symptoms of pain, swelling and heaviness.

'To follow the Tao is

To honour its principles

To realize that we live in Nature

But can never own it;

We can guide and serve

But never dominate.

This is the highest wisdom.' (Tao 51)

In Chinese medicine, there are six climatic conditions that are thought to be potential causes of disease. They are: wind, cold, dampness, fire, dryness and summer heat. For an individual with harmoniously balanced Yin and Yang energies, these weather conditions are just natural phenomena and have no detrimental effects. A person only becomes susceptible to an invasion of these factors if they are weakened by a loss of equilibrium between Yin and Yang. When this is the case, the Zhen Qi, or upright Qi *(see page 18)*, which makes up the body's immune defence system,

External pathogenic factors

	General characteristics	Typical symptoms	Examples of disease
Wind	Yang by nature. Suddenly arises and rapidly changes. Is constantly moving, upwards and outwards. Moves in gusts.	Pain that moves from place to place. Itching, skin eruptions, twitching, tremors, spasms and aversion to wind.	Common cold, urticaria, epilepsy, Parkinson's disease, facial paralysis.
Cold	Yin by nature. Causes contraction and stagnation. Consumes Yang Qi.	Symptoms that are worse for cold and better for warmth. Severe biting pain and contracted tendons. Watery, clear or white bodily discharges.	Period pains, vomiting, common cold, epigastric or abdominal pain, diarrhoea, cold hands and feet.
Damp	Yin by nature. Sticky, turbid, viscous. Heavy with tendency to descend. Causes obstruction and stagnation. Easily turns into phlegm and injures the spleen.	Fixed pain. Symptoms of heaviness and tiredness. Loss of appetite, diarrhoea, vaginal discharge, cloudy urine, swelling and fullness of the chest and abdomen.	Rheumatism, arthritis, eczema, thrush, diarrhoea, cold sores.
Dryness	Yang by nature. Consumes body fluids. Injures blood and lungs.	Dehydration, thirst, scanty urine, dry constipated stools, dry cough and dry mouth, lips, skin, throat, and nose.	Constipation, some skin conditions, cough.
Summer heat	Yang by nature. Moves upwards. Dries body fluids. Exhausts Yin and Qi. Disturbs the mind.	High fever, sweating, redness, feelings of heat, thirst, dark scanty urine, thick yellow mucus, dark dry stools, constipation and restlessness.	Sore throat, sunstroke, dysentery, tonsillitis, conjunctivitis, boils, ulcers.
Fire	Yang by nature. Utmost heat. Consumes body fluids. Injures the spirit.	Dehydration, haemorrhage, delirium, convulsion, coma.	Severe feverish conditions.

Miscellaneous causes

These are all other causes that do not fall into the categories of internal emotional or external pathogenic causes. Weak constitution, traumatic injury, parasites and poisons, wrong treatment and environmental pollution are all possible causes of disease. Generally speaking, miscellaneous causes are mainly connected to lifestyle such as a poor diet, lack of exercise, overwork of a mental or physical nature and excessive sexual activity. The rule of thumb to maintain balance and health seems to be: take everything in moderation and nothing in excess. For a more detailed account on the causes of disease in Chinese medicine, consult one of the texts on theory listed under Resources (see page 139).

Eight Guiding Principles

*Ba Gang – the Chinese characters
for the eight guiding principles*

The eight guiding principles – Ba Gang – are born from the root theory of Chinese medicine: Yin and Yang. The concept of Yin Yang theory is too universal to identify patterns of disharmony using it alone, so a further system of classification is needed. The eight principles include Yin and Yang, plus six other sub-divisions of paired opposites which represent the fundamental qualities of Yin and Yang. These are: hot and cold, interior and exterior, deficiency and excess. This provides a clearer framework for identifying patterns of disharmony and formulating appropriate treatment principles.

Any variety of symptoms can be gathered together according to the eight principles. For example, fever, aversion to cold, body aches and a superficial pulse are all symptoms of an exterior pattern. A red face, strong thirst, restlessness and a red tongue are symptoms of a heat pattern.

After gathering together all the signs and symptoms expressed by an individual, the practitioner is able to see the basic patterns that are manifesting and can formulate simple sentences to describe these. The case history *(right)* illustrates this.

The tables over the following three pages show how symptoms are grouped within the framework of the eight principles. However, these are not neat pigeon holes but rather guide the practitioner towards an understanding of the disharmony in an individual. It is good to be aware that in practice you often find combined patterns such as a pattern of interior deficient heat plus exterior excess cold. Patterns can be hot and cold, Yin and Yang, deficient and excess at the same time. *(For more detailed information on the eight guiding principles, see Further reading, page 139.)*

Case history

Name Maria

Age 28 years

Symptoms

Maria has dull epigastric (upper belly) pain which feels better when she lies down with a hot-water bottle on her belly. She easily feels cold, is often tired, has a pale complexion, poor appetite and loose stools. She has a pale, swollen tongue and a weak, deep, slow pulse.

Diagnosis

Forming a simple sentence we would say that this is an interior deficient cold pattern of disharmony. From here the practitioner needs to assess which of the organs are being affected. In this case, we could expand our sentence to say this is a stomach and spleen deficient and cold pattern of disharmony. The symptoms of deficiency are: pain that is better for lying down, tiredness, dull pain, poor appetite, loose stools, pale complexion, weak pulse and pale swollen tongue. The symptoms of cold are: pain that is better for warmth, easily feeling cold and slow pulse. The epigastric pain points to the stomach and the poor appetite, loose stools, and swollen tongue to the spleen.

Treatment

The treatment principle for this case history would be: tonify and warm the stomach and spleen.

Exterior patterns of disharmony

These are characterized by sudden onset and short duration of symptoms, aversion to wind or cold, body aches, stiff neck, fever, stuffy nose and sweating.
There are four patterns: *exterior heat, exterior cold, exterior excess and exterior deficiency.*

	Symptoms	Tongue	Pulse	Treatment principle
Exterior heat	Fever, thirst, sore throat, some sweating, aversion to cold.	Coating thin and yellow, tongue body red	Superficial or floating and rapid	Release the exterior (induce sweating).
Exterior cold	Strong aversion to cold, distinct body aches, headache, chills, slight or no fever, no sweating, no thirst.	Moist with a thin white coating	Superficial or floating and tight	Release the exterior (induce sweating).
Exterior excess	Fever, aversion to cold, distinct body aches, no sweating.	Thin white or yellow coating	Superficial or floating and tight	Release the exterior (induce sweating).
Exterior deficiency	Slight or no fever, sweating, aversion to wind, slight or no body aches.	Thin coating	Superficial or floating and slow or moderate	Harmonize the nutritive *Ying* Qi and defensive *Wei* Qi.

Interior patterns of disharmony

These are characterized by prolonged symptoms, no fever or fever with no chills.
There are four patterns: *interior heat, interior cold, interior excess and interior deficiency.*

	Symptoms	Tongue	Pulse	Treatment principle
Interior heat	Red face, red eyes, red raised skin eruptions, aversion to heat, thirst for cold drinks, dark urine, stools that are dry and hard, constipated or foul smelling diarrhoea, burning sensation at the anus or urethra, extreme restlessness, irregular menstrual cycle with scanty or copious bright or dark red blood and red clots.	Red body and yellow coating	Rapid and overflowing	Clear heat.
Interior cold	Pale white complexion, chilliness, aversion to cold, cold extremities, no thirst or thirst for only warm drinks, pain which is better for warmth, loose stools, clear copious urine. Distended abdomen, pain worse for pressure and better for evacuation, feelings of fullness, constipation.	Pale, white coating	Deep, slow and tight	Warm the interior and scatter cold.

	Symptoms	Tongue	Pulse	Treatment principle
Interior excess	Abdominal distension, pain worse for pressure and better for evacuation, feelings of fullness, constipation.	Thick, greasy, sticky coating	Full, deep, slippery and wiry	Quell, subdue, resolve the excess.
Interior deficiency	Pale face, tiredness, weakness, pain better for pressure and for eating and worse for evacuation, poor appetite, weak voice, thin constipated forceless stools, dizziness, spontaneous sweating, palpitations, dribbling urine, early or no periods.	Thin or absent coating	Deep, thready, weak	Strengthen, tonify, supplement.

Patterns of disharmony associated with heat

These are characterized by feelings of heat or fever, sweating and thirst.
There are four patterns: *exterior heat, interior heat, excess heat and deficient heat*.
We have already covered exterior and interior heat. Below are the other two.

	Symptoms	Tongue	Pulse	Treatment principle
Excess heat	High fever, sweating, restlessness, thirst for cold drinks, confusion, distended abdomen, constipation or foul-smelling diarrhoea, burning pain, worse for pressure, dark yellow scanty urine, red eyes, red face, heavy periods with bright red or dark clotted blood.	Red with yellow coating	Rapid and overflowing	Clear heat, drain or quell fire.
Deficient heat	A feeling of heat in the afternoon, night sweating, a feeling of heat in the chest, palms of hands and soles of feet, dry mouth and throat, emaciation.	Red with a thin or absent coating	Thready, rapid	Nourish Yin, clear empty heat.

Patterns of disharmony associated with cold

These are characterized by aversion to cold, lack of thirst and pale face.
There are four patterns: *exterior cold, interior cold, excess cold and deficient cold*.
We have covered exterior and interior cold. Below are the other two.

	Symptoms	Tongue	Pulse	Treatment principle
Excess cold	Pale face, aversion to cold, chilliness, better for warmth, cold limbs, no thirst or only for warm drinks, pain that is fixed and sharp, worse for pressure and cold, loose stools, pale copious urine.	Pale, thick, white coating	Full and tight	Warm the interior and scatter cold.

	Symptoms	Tongue	Pulse	Treatment principle
Deficient cold	Aversion to cold, cold limbs, face pale and drained, loose stools or diarrhoea with no smell, frequent pale copious urine, spontaneous sweating.	Swollen and pale with thin, white, slimy coating	Thready, weak	Warm and tonify Yang.

Patterns of disharmony associated with deficiency

These are characterized by feelings of weakness, tiredness.
There are six patterns: *deficient cold, deficient heat, deficient Qi, deficient blood, deficient Yin and deficient Yang.*
We have covered deficient cold and heat. Below are the remaining four.

	Symptoms	Tongue	Pulse	Treatment principle
Deficient Qi	Cold weak limbs, tiredness, dizziness, feels better for eating, for pressure and for rest and feels worse for activity and for evacuation, spontaneous sweating, breathlessness on exertion, no appetite, loose stools or forceless constipation, dribbling urine.	Quivering, swollen, pale with thin white coating	Weak, thready	Tonify Qi.
Deficient Blood	Dizziness, fainting, dry eyes, blurred vision, scanty periods with thin watery blood, stiffness, pale face, numbness, pale lips.	Pale	Choppy	Nourish blood.
Deficient Yin	Red cheeks, night sweats, feeling of heat in chest, palms of hands and soles of feet, dry cough, frequent dark scanty urine, lower back ache, hard stools, insomnia, periods come with dark or bright red blood, thirst for cold drinks or to sip warm drinks.	Red with a thin, peeled coating	Thready and rapid	Nourish Yin.
Deficient Yang	Pale white face, cold limbs, bluish colour to face and lips, weakness, aversion to cold, diarrhoea, thin body, spontaneous sweating, frequent pale copious dribbling urine.	Pale, swollen	Weak, slowish	Warm and tonify Yang.

Patterns of disharmony associated with excess

These are characterized by feelings of fullness, pain that is worse for pressure and restlessness.
There are four patterns: *exterior excess, interior excess, excess heat and excess cold.*
The signs and symptoms for these patterns have been covered in the tables given.

Making a Diagnosis

A practitioner of any branch of traditional Chinese medicine, including Tui Na, must find the pattern or patterns of a person's disharmony and make a diagnosis before deciding on a treatment. This is where all the building blocks of the theory, such as the eight guiding principles and the functions of the internal organs, come together.

When someone comes for treatment, the practitioner has to gather as much information about them as possible. Everything must be taken into consideration, from the overall manner and body type to the texture and colour of the skin, from the quality of the pulse to the emotional state and the look of the tongue. All the signs and symptoms are written down in the form of a case history.

No individual symptom or sign is viewed in isolation – it is only when everything is viewed together that a picture begins to form and the patterns of disharmony emerge. For instance, a red tone to the skin could indicate a pattern of excess heat or deficient heat. It is only when other symptoms and signs are brought into the picture that it becomes clear: a red tone to the skin, a feeling of tiredness in the afternoon, night sweats, a thin body, a thready rapid pulse and a dry, thin tongue body with a peeled coating. All of these together point clearly to a pattern of deficient heat.

Gathering information

A practitioner finds the information that he or she needs by making four examinations of the patient. These are: examination by looking, examination by asking, examination by listening and smelling, and examination by feeling. Over the next few pages is a brief outline of each of the four examinations, emphasizing the most important elements. *(For more detailed information, see Further reading, page 139.)*

Examine by looking

First of all, as the practitioner, you need to look for any signs and symptoms. Observe the patient's general body shape, gestures, overall manner, spirit, the colour and texture of the skin, the eyes, ears, nose, mouth and lips, hair, teeth and gums, and the body and coating of the tongue. Over the next two pages is a table giving a few examples of how what is observed can be classified in terms of the principles of Chinese medicine.

Tongue diagnosis

Observation of the tongue is of vital importance in making a diagnosis and gives clear information about an individual's underlying disharmony, even in the most complex cases. The tongue is observed for its colour, shape, moisture and coating. Refer to the chart *(opposite and overleaf)* to see what these signs can indicate in terms of Chinese medicine. Different areas of the tongue also relate to different organs, as shown below. For example a very red tongue tip can indicate heat in the heart; a thick yellow greasy tongue coating in the centre of the tongue is a sign of damp heat in the stomach and spleen; a purplish tongue body at the sides indicates stagnation of liver Qi.

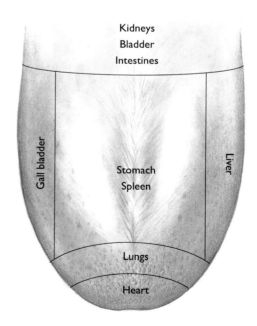

Division of the tongue

Different areas on the tongue relate to different internal organs. Note the shape, colour, coating and moisture in each area to relate to the information in the chart opposite and overleaf.

Examination by looking

	Observed signs	What they might indicate
Body shape	Thin body	Yin deficiency, blood deficiency
	Overweight	Qi deficiency, Yang deficiency, damp
	Weak looking	Deficient patterns likely
	Strong looking	Excess patterns likely
Movements and gestures	Jerky fast movements	Excess patterns, heat
	Lack of movement or slow movements	Deficient patterns, cold
	Tremors	Wind
Skin colour	Greenish tint	Liver pattern, interior cold, wind, wood element disharmony
	Red tint	Excess heat, deficient heat, fire element disharmony
	Yellow tint	Spleen deficiency, damp, earth element disharmony
	White tint	Yang deficiency, blood deficiency, cold, metal element disharmony
	Dull/pale/white	Blood deficiency
	Bright white	Yang deficiency
	Black tint	Cold, kidney Yin deficiency, blood stagnation, water element disharmony
Skin texture	Dry skin	Yin deficiency, blood deficiency
	Flaky skin	Yin deficiency, blood deficiency, phlegm
	Greasy skin	Damp, phlegm
	Spotty skin	Excess patterns, heat, damp or phlegm
	Oedema	Excess body fluids
Eyes	Clear and glittering	Good vitality, strong spirit and essence
	Swelling under the eyes	Kidney deficiency
	Corners of eyes red	Kidney deficiency
	Sclera (white of eye) red	Lung heat
	Sclera yellow	Damp heat
	Whole eye red and swollen	Invasion of wind heat or liver fire
	Dry eyes	Blood deficiency
	Jerky eye movements	Liver pattern

Tongue diagnosis

	Observed signs	What they might indicate
Colour *A normal tongue body is pale red*	Pale	Yang deficiency, especially if swollen and wet, or blood deficiency
	Very red	Excess heat if coating is present, or deficient heat if no coating
	Purple	Stasis of blood. If purple at sides, liver blood stasis. If purple in centre, blood stasis in stomach
	Reddish purple	Stasis of blood and heat
	Bluish purple	Stasis of blood and cold
	Blue	Interior cold and blood stasis

31

	Observed signs	What they might indicate
Shape	Swollen	Retention of damp. If it is also pale, Yang deficiency
	Stiff	Interior wind
	Thin	If pale, blood deficiency. If red, Yin deficiency
	Flaccid	Deficient body fluids
	Short	If pale and wet, interior cold. If red with a peeled coating, Yin deficiency
	Long	Heat in the heart
	Quivering	Spleen deficiency
	Cracked	Excess heat or deficient Yin
	Crack along the midline to tip	Heart pattern
	Crack along the midline in the centre	Stomach Yin deficiency or stomach Qi deficiency
	Short transverse crack in middle of sides	Spleen Qi deficiency
	Horizontal cracks	Yin deficiency
	Deviated	Interior wind
Coating *A normal tongue coating is thin and white*	Thick coating	Excess pattern. Pathogenic factor such as wind, damp, cold, heat
	No coating	Stomach Yin deficiency, kidney Yin deficiency
	White coating	Cold (unless thin and white)
	Yellow coating	Excess heat
	Grey/black coating	If wet, indicates extreme cold. If dry, indicates extreme heat
Moisture *A normal tongue is slightly moist*	Very wet	Damp, Yang deficiency
	Dry with coating	Excess heat
	Dry without coating	Deficient heat
	Sticky, greasy	Phlegm, damp

Examine by asking

Next is the examination by asking. First ask about the main complaint, health and family history, and present circumstances, such as work, relationships and children. This is to find the cause of the ailment, so that dietary and lifestyle advice can be given that will aid recovery and prevent the problem recurring. Then you can begin more specific questioning aimed at finding the pattern of disharmony. The questions depend largely on the ailment itself, but the list opposite should help.

The tables over the next two pages give an idea of how different signs and symptoms can be related to theory. It is by no means extensive but, if you understand the eight principles, the functions of the internal organs and the causes of disease, you will be able to take signs and symptoms and work out the pattern of disharmony. This of course takes time and a good deal of practice.

What questions to ask

- *Sleep* Quality? Quantity? Dreams?
- *Food* Appetite? Digestion? Diet?
- *Thirst* Thirsty or not? How much is drunk? Desire for hot or cold drinks?
- *Stools* Regularity? Consistency? Colour? Smell? Pain?
- *Urine* Quantity? Colour? Frequency? Smell? Pain?
- *Temperature* Feel hot or cold? Dislike heat or cold?
- *Pains* Where? When? Better or worse for pressure, heat, movement, rest? Pain in chest, rib area or belly?
- *Head* Headaches: where on the head, time of day, type of pain? Vision and hearing: blurred vision, tinnitus?
- *Sweating* What time of day or night? How much?
- *Women* Menstruation: regularity, colour, quantity of blood, clots, pain, emotions? Discharge: colour and consistency? Pregnancy and childbirth: how many children, birth, post birth, miscarriages?

Diagnosis from asking questions

	Signs and symptoms	What they might indicate
Sleep	Difficulty falling asleep	Heart blood deficiency
	Waking up during the night	Heart and/or kidney Yin deficiency
	Sleep disturbed by dreams	Liver or heart fire
	Waking up early and unable to get back to sleep	Gall bladder deficiency
	Extremely restless sleep	Phlegm fire harassing the heart
Food	No appetite or low appetite	Spleen Qi deficiency
	Constantly hungry	Stomach fire
	Hungry but can't eat much	Retention of phlegm heat
	Feeling bloated after eating	Spleen Qi deficiency, damp, retention of food
	Wants hot food	Interior cold
	Wants cold food	Interior heat
Thirst	Thirst for a large amount of cold water	Excess heat
	No thirst	Cold pattern
	Thirst, but no desire to drink	Damp heat
	Thirst, with desire to slowly sip warm drinks	Stomach or kidney Yin deficiency
Stools	Feels worse after passing stools	Deficient pattern
	Feels better after passing stools	Excess pattern
	Infrequent, dry, hard stools	Heat, Qi deficiency, blood deficiency, deficiency of body fluids
	Constipation with small, compacted, bitty stools	Liver Qi stagnation, heat in the intestines
	Difficulty passing the stools but not dry	Spleen Qi deficiency, liver Qi stagnation
	Constipation plus abdominal pain, better for warmth	Deficiency of kidney Yang and interior cold
	Alternating constipation and diarrhoea	Liver Qi stagnation invading the spleen
	Foul-smelling diarrhoea	Heat
	Diarrhoea with no smell	Cold
	Chronic diarrhoea	Spleen and/or kidney Yang deficiency
	Mucus in stools	Damp in the intestines
	Dark stools	Heat
	Pale stools	Cold
Urine	Pale and abundant	Cold, Yang deficiency
	Yellow and scanty	Heat, Yin deficiency
	Cloudy	Damp
	Strong smelling	Heat
	Dribbling	Kidney deficiency
Epigastrium *(Upper belly)*	Severe pain	Excess pattern
	Dull pain	Deficient pattern
	Better after eating	Deficient pattern
	Worse after eating	Excess pattern
	Feeling of fullness	Damp, spleen Qi deficiency

ES102

	Signs and symptoms	What they might indicate
Pain	Better with pressure	Deficient pattern
	Worse with pressure	Excess pattern
	Better for warmth	Cold pattern
	Better for cold	Hot pattern
	Stabbing pain	Blood stasis
	Burning pain	Heat
	Cold pain	Cold
	Distending pain	Stagnation of Qi
Menstruation	Short cycle with profuse deep red blood	Heat, excess pattern
	Long cycle, scanty light coloured blood	Cold, deficiency pattern
	Irregular cycle	Liver Qi stagnation or spleen deficiency
	Long cycle, purplish blood and clots	Stagnation of blood
	Watery, scanty pale blood	Blood deficiency
	Pain before period	Blood or Qi stagnation
	Pain during period	Stagnation of cold, Qi and blood or heat
	Pain after period	Blood deficiency

Examine by hearing and smelling

The practitioner must also listen to the sound of the patient's voice, their breathing and any other sounds they may be making, such as coughing, hiccuping and gurgling. In general, any loud sounds indicate an excess pattern and any weak quiet sounds point to a pattern of deficiency. The theory of the five elements can be used to assess the quality of someone's voice (*see page 14 for the table of correspondences*).

Strong smells, such as foul-smelling stools, are a sign of heat, and a complete lack of smell is a sign of cold. General body smells such as sweet, rancid and burnt can indicate disharmony of the internal organs. Again, refer to the five elements theory for correspondences.

Examine by feeling

This is the final examination, where you, as the practitioner, must feel various parts of the patient's body in order to gather further information regarding the nature of their disharmony. The skin may be felt for temperature and moisture; the limbs for swelling, temperature, areas of tightness or flaccidity; and the abdomen for areas of fullness and emptiness.

Pulse diagnosis

The most important aspect of the feeling examination is pulse diagnosis. By feeling the individual's pulse, a practitioner can gather a huge amount of information about the state of the internal organs, the Qi and blood, and the balance of Yin and Yang. However, pulse diagnosis is extremely difficult to learn. It is a subtle art requiring incredible sensitivity which can only develop through years of practice feeling pulse after pulse.

There are twenty-eight different pulse qualities, such as thready, wiry, slippery, rapid, floating, slow and deep. All these provide vital information. It is nigh on impossible to learn pulse diagnosis from a book, but if you wish to try feeling the pulse qualities of your partner, friends and family, the most important factor to ascertain-is whether the pulse reflects an excess or a deficient condition. The descriptions opposite offer a few of the main pulse qualities.

How is the pulse felt?

The person whose pulse you are feeling should be relaxed, either lying down or sitting, with their arm horizontal. Any watches or jewellery must be removed from the wrist. Feel the radial artery pulse – this is on the radius-side of the wrist – with your index, middle and ring fingers. Feel the pulse on both wrists, in three positions and at three levels, as described below.

Pulse positions

The pulse is felt in three positions. The front position on the left wrist reflects the state of the heart and chest; on the right it reflects the lungs and chest. The middle position on the left wrist reflects the liver and gall bladder; on the right the stomach and spleen. The rear position on the left reflects the kidneys, bladder and small intestine; on the right the kidneys and large intestine.

Pulse levels

The pulse is felt on three levels. The first is superficial, which is felt by gently resting the fingers on the pulse; this reflects the state of the individual's Qi. The middle level is felt with a moderate pressure and reflects the state of the individual's blood. The deep level is felt using quite strong pressure and reflects the state of the individual's Yin.

Feeling the pulse

The patient's arm should be horizontal and no higher than the level of the heart. Place your fingers on the radial artery pulse (on the thumb-side of the inner wrist) and feel with your index, middle and ring fingers, first with light pressure, then medium, then quite strong.

Pulse diagnosis

Pulse qualities	Signs and symptoms	What they might indicate
Floating or superficial	Feels strong under very gentle pressure and loses its strength under deeper pressure	An invasion of an exterior pathogenic factor
Deep	This can only be felt under strong pressure near the bone	An interior pattern
Slow	Pulse beats only 3 times per breath of practitioner	A cold pattern
Rapid	Beats six times per breath of practitioner	A heat pattern
Empty	Feels big and soft and becomes empty on deeper pressure	Qi deficiency
Full	Feels big and strong and can be felt on all levels	An excess pattern
Slippery	Feels smooth and round, and slides under the fingers	Presence of phlegm, damp or retention of food
Wiry	Feels strong, taut and hard, and hits the fingers	Disharmony of the liver, phlegm or that the patient is in pain
Thready	Feels soft, weak and lacking in strength	Blood deficiency and/or Qi deficiency

Meridians

Qi can be absorbed into the human body via portals of entry on the skin. These are called points, and they are stimulated with Tui Na and acupuncture. It helps to see them as doorways which open into a system called the Jingluo. 'Jing' means 'route' or 'to move through'; 'Luo' means 'net'. The Jingluo – or meridians – are channels formed into a network along which Qi and blood flow. The vital substances that flow through the meridian network provide life-giving and life-sustaining energy to every part of a human being. It is this network that connects everything in the body. This is important in understanding how a treatment like Tui Na works. By stimulating points on the exterior of the body, we can create changes inside.

The meridian network consists of twelve primary channels. Each one hooks up internally with an organ, whose name it carries. The Yin channels hook up to the Zang Yin organs and the Yang channels to the Fu Yang organs. Therefore, we have six primary Yin channels and six primary Yang channels.

These primary meridians can be paired up so that each Yang meridian is paired with a Yin meridian *(as shown in the diagram, right)*. The lung meridian pairs with the large intestine meridian, pericardium with triple burner, heart with small intestine, spleen with stomach, and so on.

There are also eight extra meridians. Only two of these have points of their own – the governing vessel and the conception vessel. The others all share points with meridians which coincide with their pathway.

On the next pages, you will find pictures showing the pathways of each of the twelve primary meridians, plus the governing vessel and conception vessel. Points that are referred to in the points table *(see pages 48–53)* are all labelled on their relevant meridians. Each meridian travels over the surface of the skin for part of its length, but also has branches which travel internally. Some of the simpler internal pathways are included here, to give you an indication of the ways in which meridians relate to internal organs and each other. Remember that, although they are shown here only on one side of the body, all the meridians run symmetrically on both sides of the body.

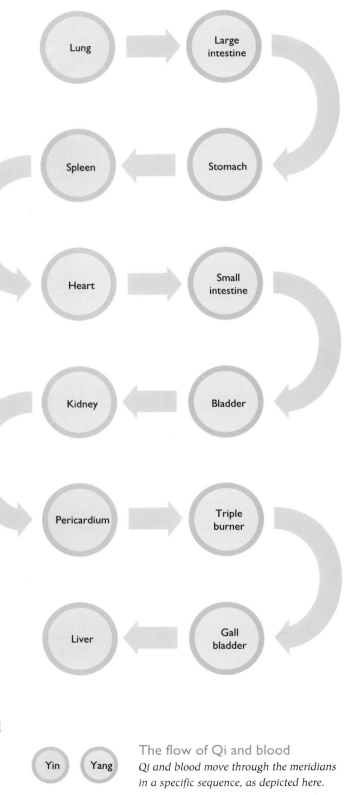

The flow of Qi and blood
Qi and blood move through the meridians in a specific sequence, as depicted here.

Lung meridian (Lu)

Tai Yin

— Meridian on
surface of skin

····· Internal meridian

● Key points

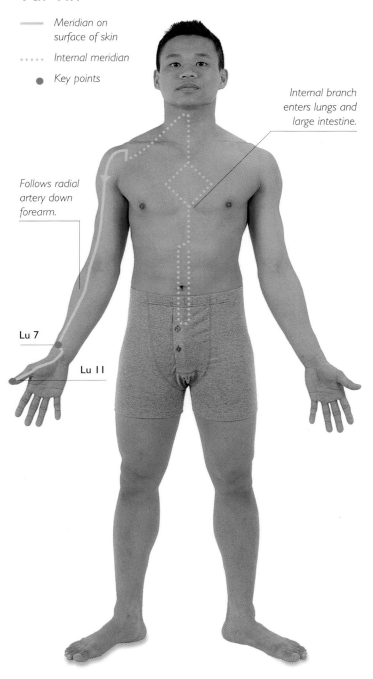

Internal branch
enters lungs and
large intestine.

Follows radial
artery down
forearm.

Lu 7

Lu 11

The lung meridian begins in middle burner and travels
internally through large intestine and lungs. It emerges
below collar bone and terminates at the lateral corner of
the thumb nail, where the nail starts. A separate branch
(not shown) connects the lung meridian with the first
point of the large intestine meridian.

Large intestine meridian (LI)

Yang Ming

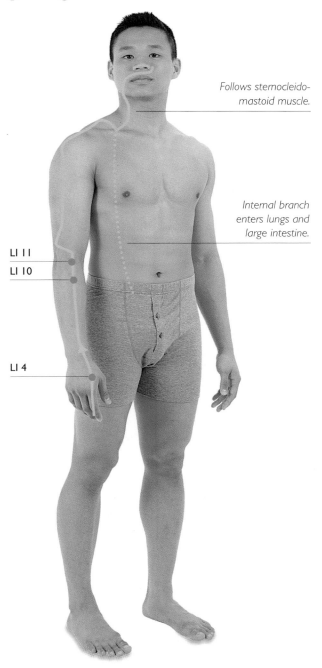

Follows sternocleido-
mastoid muscle.

Internal branch
enters lungs and
large intestine.

LI 11

LI 10

LI 4

The large intestine meridian begins at the nail corner of
the index finger and passes up the front of the arm. It
then travels down into the supraclavicular fossa. From
here, one branch descends internally to the lungs and
large intestine. The external branch continues upwards
to terminate at the side of the nose.

Stomach meridian (St)

Yang Ming

St 8

Internal branch enters
stomach and spleen.

Emerges under the eye.

St 25

St 28

St 29

St 36

St 40

St 44

St 45

The stomach meridian begins internally where the large
intestine meridian finishes, and emerges under the eye.
It moves down to the supraclavicular fossa, where one
branch descends internally, entering the stomach and
spleen. The external meridian terminates at the nail of
the second toe, with a separate branch (not shown)
connecting with the first point of the spleen meridian.

Spleen meridian (Sp)

Tai Yin

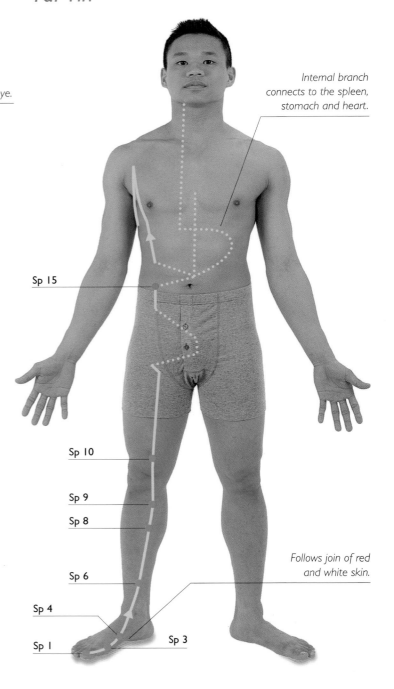

Internal branch
connects to the spleen,
stomach and heart.

Sp 15

Sp 10

Sp 9

Sp 8

Sp 6

Follows join of red
and white skin.

Sp 4

Sp 1

Sp 3

The spleen meridian begins on the medial side of the
nail of the big toe and runs along the foot at the join
of the red and white skin. It then travels up inside of
leg and front of torso. An internal branch runs to the
spleen, stomach and heart. Another internal branch
follows the throat to the base of the tongue.

Heart meridian (Ht)

Shao Yin

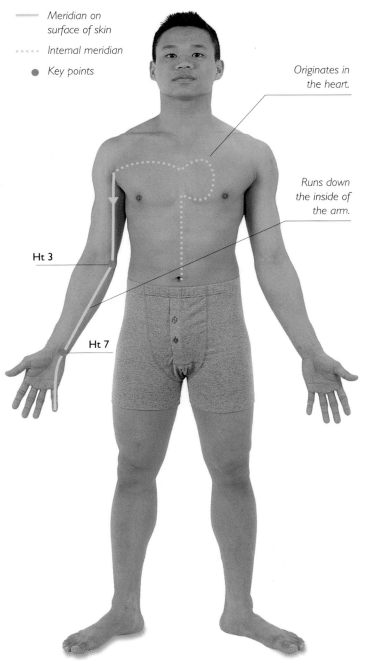

— Meridian on surface of skin

····· Internal meridian

● Key points

Originates in the heart.

Runs down the inside of the arm.

Ht 3

Ht 7

The heart meridian originates in the heart. One branch descends to the small intestine, another emerges at the armpit. It travels externally down the arm and terminates at the medial nail corner of the little finger, connecting with small intestine meridian.

Small intestine meridian (SI)

Tai Yang

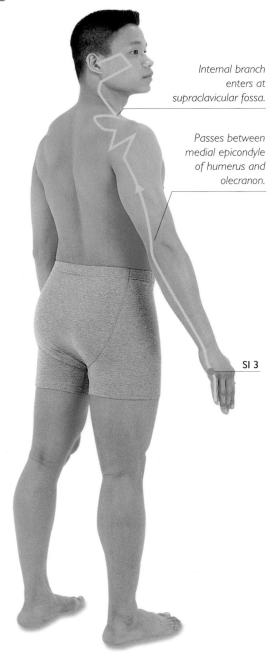

Internal branch enters at supraclavicular fossa.

Passes between medial epicondyle of humerus and olecranon.

SI 3

The small intestine meridian begins at the lateral nail corner of the little finger. It travels up the back of the arm and over the shoulder into the supraclavicular fossa. An internal branch descends to the small intestine, while the main branch ascends the neck and connects with the bladder meridian at the inner canthus of the eye.

Bladder meridian (Bl)

Tai Yang

'Back transporting points' run parallel to the spine.

Internal branch to kidney and bladder.

Bl 13
Bl 15
Bl 17
Bl 18
Bl 20
Bl 22
Bl 25
Bl 36
Bl 40
Bl 60

Bl 21
Bl 23

The bladder meridian starts at the inner canthus of the eye. It crosses the crown of the head and travels in parallel branches down the back. An internal branch connects to the kidney and descends to the bladder. The meridian terminates at the lateral nail corner of the little toe, connecting with the kidney meridian.

Kidney meridian (Ki)

Shao Yin

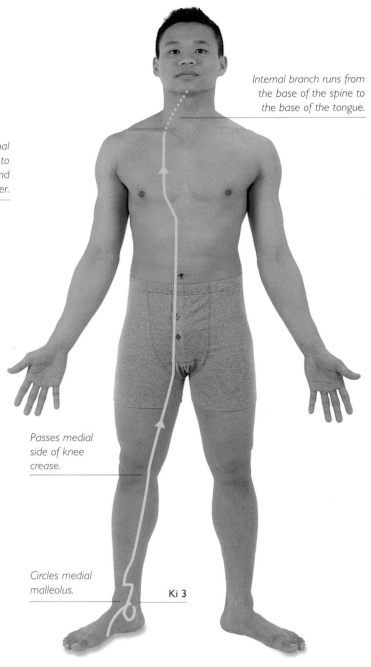

Internal branch runs from the base of the spine to the base of the tongue.

Passes medial side of knee crease.

Circles medial malleolus.

Ki 3

The kidney meridian begins under the little toe and travels under the foot. It ascends the inside of leg and up the torso to the collar bone. An internal branch penetrates the body near the base of the spine and continues upwards, connecting with the kidney, bladder, heart and pericardium, to the base of the tongue.

Pericardium meridian (P)

Jue Yin

— Meridian on surface of skin

····· Internal meridian

● Key points

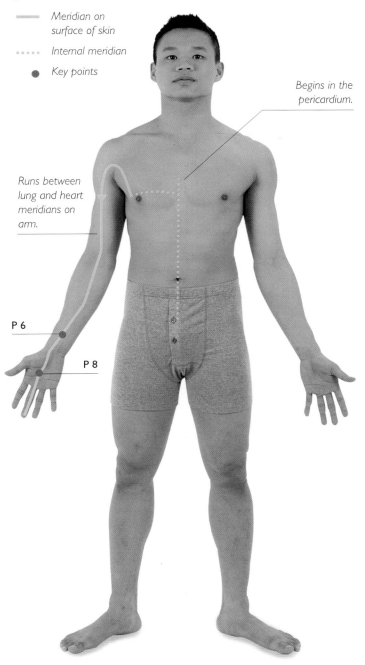

Begins in the pericardium.

Runs between lung and heart meridians on arm.

P 6

P 8

The pericardium meridian begins in the pericardium and descends through the upper, middle and lower burners. It emerges near the nipple and travels down the arm to terminate at the tip of the little finger. Another internal branch (not shown) runs from P 8 to connect with the first point of the triple burner meridian.

Triple burner meridian (TB)

Shao Yang

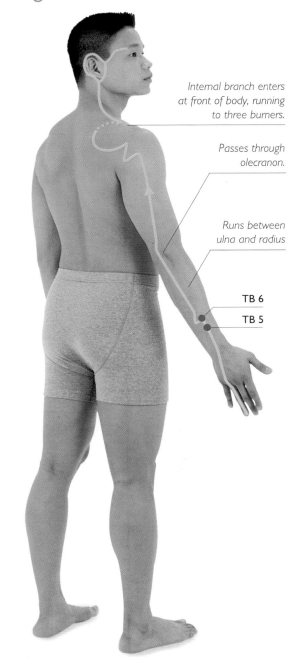

Internal branch enters at front of body, running to three burners.

Passes through olecranon.

Runs between ulna and radius

TB 6
TB 5

The triple burner meridian begins at the lateral nail corner of the ring finger. It travels up the arm into the supraclavicular fossa, where it descends internally into the chest to connect with the pericardium and the upper, middle and lower burners. Another branch travels up the neck and connects with the gall bladder meridian at the end of the eyebrow.

Gall bladder meridian (GB)

Shao Yang

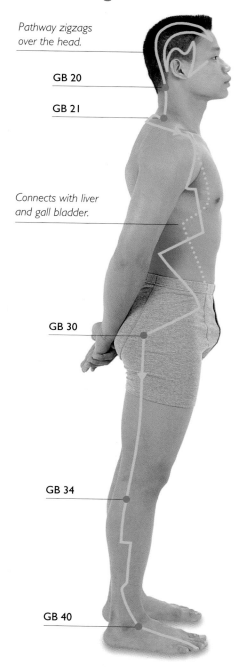

Pathway zigzags over the head.

GB 20

GB 21

Connects with liver and gall bladder.

GB 30

GB 34

GB 40

The gall bladder meridian begins at the outer canthus of the eye. It then moves downwards to supraclavicular fossa, where a branch descends internally. The main branch descends the side of the body to terminate at the nail corner of the fourth toe. A separate internal branch (not shown) connects with the first point of the liver meridian.

Liver meridian (Liv)

Jue Yin

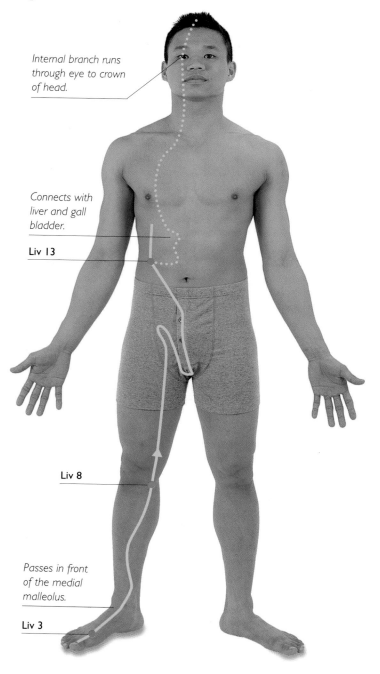

Internal branch runs through eye to crown of head.

Connects with liver and gall bladder.

Liv 13

Liv 8

Passes in front of the medial malleolus.

Liv 3

The liver meridian begins on the big toe at the corner of the nail. It travels up the inside of the leg and front of the torso, entering the abdomen. The internal branch connects with the liver and gall bladder, and ascends through the diaphragm and lungs to the throat and head.

Conception vessel (CV)

Governing vessel (GV)

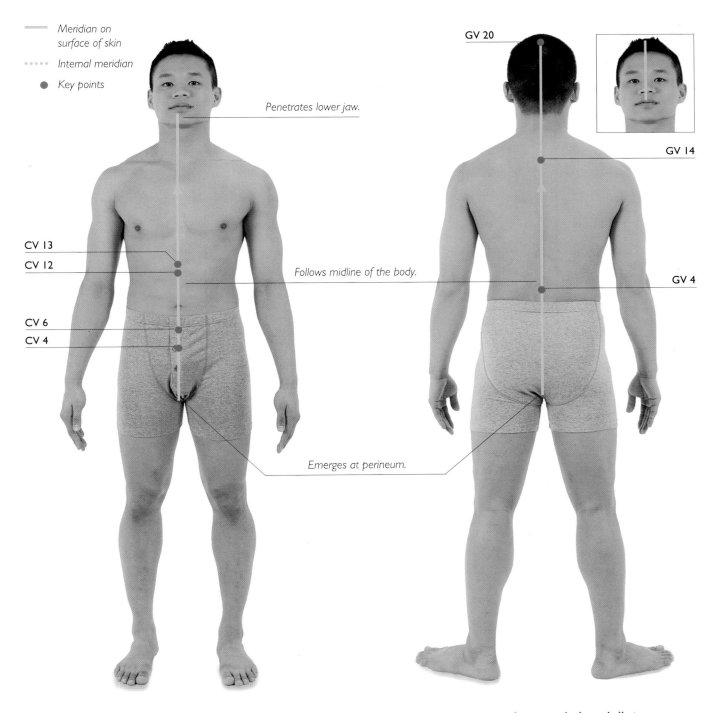

— Meridian on
surface of skin

····· Internal meridian

● Key points

Penetrates lower jaw.

GV 20

GV 14

CV 13
CV 12

Follows midline of the body.

GV 4

CV 6
CV 4

Emerges at perineum.

The conception vessel starts in the lower belly in men
and the uterus in women, and emerges at the perineum
(between the the anus and external genitalia). It follows
the anterior midline of the body to penetrate the body
at the lower jaw. The interior branch (not shown) then
encircles the lips and connects with the stomach
meridian under the eyes.

The governing vessel starts in the lower belly in
men and the uterus in women, and emerges at the
perineum. An internal branch (not shown) connects
to the kidney. The main branch follows the posterior
midline of the body to the crown and descends the
face to the upper lip.

Finding Points

There are over three hundred points on the body, but we shall concern ourselves here with fifty-seven of the most commonly used points. On pages 48–53 there is a table of all the points you will need in part three for the treatment of common ailments. The table provides a precise anatomical location for each point and a description of its actions. Western anatomical language is used for the description of where the points are found on the body

Term	Definition
Anterior	In front of
Anterior midline	Front midline of the body
Posterior	Behind
Medial	On the inside of
Lateral	On the outside of
Superior	Above
Inferior	Below
Dorsal	On the back of
Proximal	Towards the centre of the body
Distal	Away from the centre of the body
Radial	On the side of the radius
Anteriolateral	Front outside
Cubital crease	Elbow crease
Popliteal crease	Knee crease
Transverse-gluteal crease	Crease below the buttock
Thenar eminence	Ball of muscle at the base of the thumb
Axilla	Armpit
Vertex	Crown of the head
Hypochondrium	Belly
Epigastrium	Abdomen immediately over the stomach
Perineum	Area between the anus and scrotum or vulva

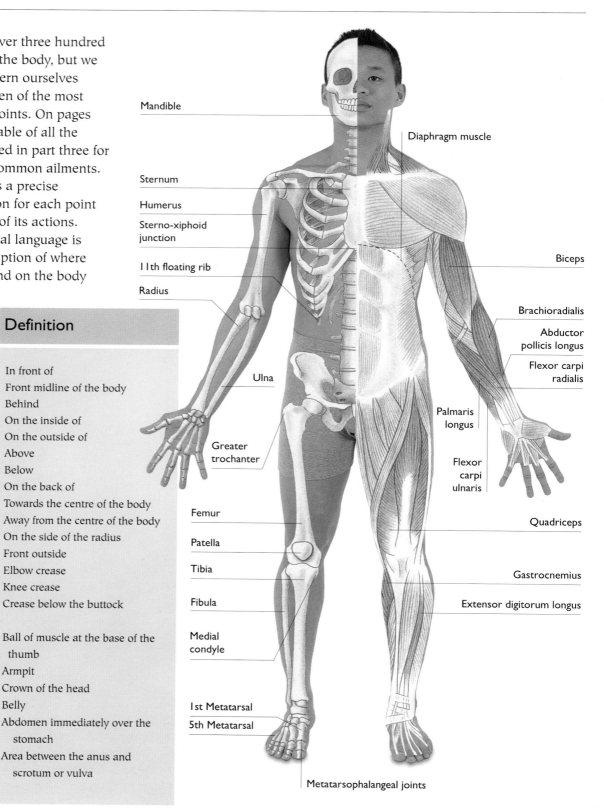

- Mandible
- Diaphragm muscle
- Sternum
- Humerus
- Sterno-xiphoid junction
- 11th floating rib
- Radius
- Biceps
- Brachioradialis
- Abductor pollicis longus
- Flexor carpi radialis
- Ulna
- Palmaris longus
- Greater trochanter
- Flexor carpi ulnaris
- Femur
- Quadriceps
- Patella
- Tibia
- Gastrocnemius
- Fibula
- Extensor digitorum longus
- Medial condyle
- 1st Metatarsal
- 5th Metatarsal
- Metatarsophalangeal joints

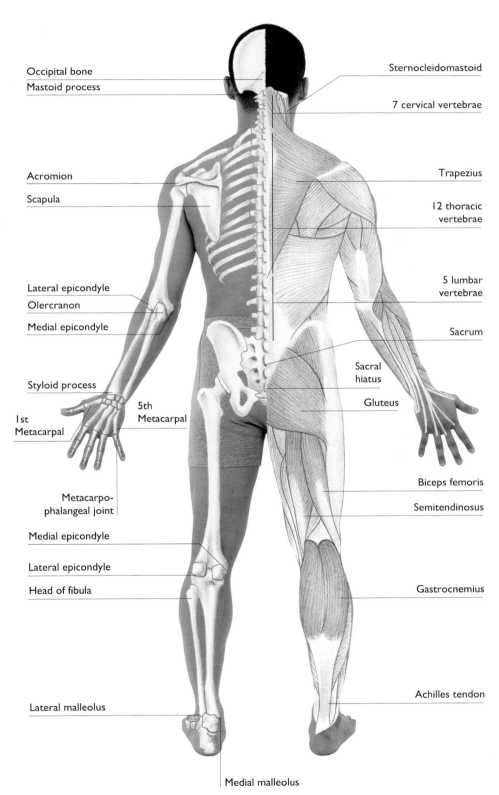

Occipital bone
Mastoid process
Acromion
Scapula
Lateral epicondyle
Olercranon
Medial epicondyle
Styloid process
5th Metacarpal
1st Metacarpal
Metacarpo-phalangeal joint
Medial epicondyle
Lateral epicondyle
Head of fibula
Lateral malleolus
Medial malleolus

Sternocleidomastoid
7 cervical vertebrae
Trapezius
12 thoracic vertebrae
5 lumbar vertebrae
Sacrum
Sacral hiatus
Gluteus
Biceps femoris
Semitendinosus
Gastrocnemius
Achilles tendon

for the purpose of accuracy. Don't be put off by the Latin names; terms such as anterior (front) and posterior (behind) are defined in the table opposite, and all the bones and muscles mentioned are clearly labelled on the diagrams here. Study these anatomical diagrams carefully and try to find the bones and muscles on your own body. Feel for your greater trochanter on your hip, and try to differentiate between the tendons on your inner wrist.

Some of the points you will need are measured by using a relative unit of measurement called cun (pronounced 'tsoon') or 'body inch'. The diagrams on page 47 show you how many cun there are – for example – from the elbow crease to the wrist crease, or from the navel to the pubic bone.

To avoid confusion, it is important to remember that a cun is not a fixed measurement – like a centimetre, for example – but a relative one. Therefore, it makes no difference if you are measuring a point on the forearm of a tiny woman or a huge man; the distance between the wrist crease and the elbow crease is always 12 cun, even though a tape measure would show the length of their forearms to be quite different.

Anatomical landmarks

The musculoskeletal information shown here is useful in the location of points, and you will find them referred to again and again in the table of key points (see pages 48–53). The important muscles are picked out in deep red. The more familiar you become with the muscles, the quicker you will be able to find points, both on yourself and others.

Measuring cun

Cun are measured by a practitioner using the hands as dividing instruments. The diagrams opposite show how the body is divided up, so you can easily locate points once you have their locations measured in cun.

I suggest that you practise measuring on as many people as you can. Go through the key points *(see pages 48–53)*. Like most things, it takes a bit of time to perfect.

When you think you have found a point, press into it with the tip of your thumb, firmly, but not roughly. You will know when you have found it by the response of your partner, who will feel it as sensitive, achy or maybe even painful. Try locating a few points on yourself – on your legs, for example – so you can experience what it feels like to have a point stimulated.

Example of point location

This example shows how to find a point 3 cun above the wrist crease. Follow the instructions here and you will be able to apply the same techniques to find other points.

Find the forearm measurement – 12 cun *(see opposite)*. Divide the forearm in half by putting the little finger of one hand on the wrist crease and the little finger of the other hand on the elbow crease. Where your index fingers meet is 6 cun. Now divide the arm from this point to the wrist crease in half in the same way.

Step one
Tuck your third and fourth fingers into your palms and bring your two index fingers to the place midway along the forearm.

Step two
Repeat the process to further divide the arm. Where your index fingers meet is 3 cun above the wrist crease.

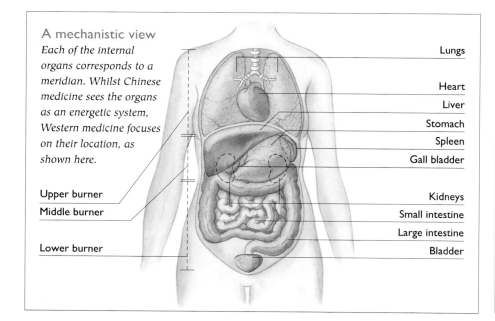

A mechanistic view
Each of the internal organs corresponds to a meridian. Whilst Chinese medicine sees the organs as an energetic system, Western medicine focuses on their location, as shown here.

Upper burner
Middle burner
Lower burner

Lungs
Heart
Liver
Stomach
Spleen
Gall bladder
Kidneys
Small intestine
Large intestine
Bladder

Tips for measuring cun

- The width of your four fingers together is 3 cun
- The length of the middle bone of your middle finger is about 1 cun
- The combined width of your index finger and middle finger is approximately 1.5 cun

NB IF USING THESE SHORT-CUT TECHNIQUES ON SOMEONE ELSE, REMEMBER TO COMPENSATE FOR THE RELATIVE SIZE DIFFERENCE BETWEEN YOUR FINGERS.

Dividing the body

Armpit to elbow crease – **9 cun**

Elbow crease to wrist crease – **12 cun**

Top of pubic bone to knee crease – **20 cun**

Greater trochanter to knee crease – **19 cun**

Knee crease to lateral malleolus – **16 cun**

Knee crease to medial malleolus – **15 cun**

Nipple to nipple – **8 cun**

Sterno-xiphoid junction to navel – **8 cun**

Navel to top of pubic bone – **5 cun**

Spine to scapula – **3 cun**

Anterior to posterior hairline – **12 cun**

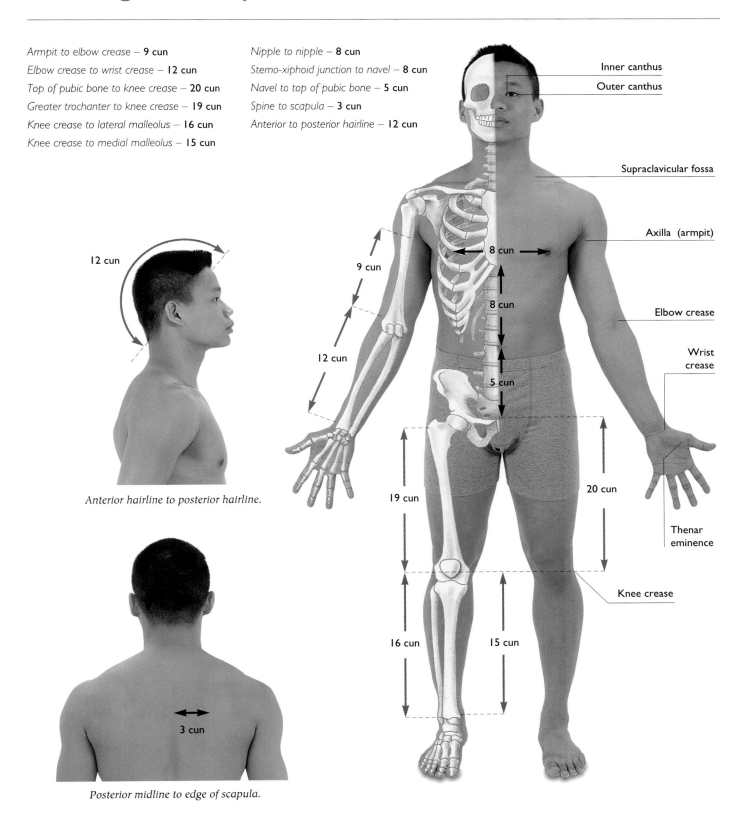

Anterior hairline to posterior hairline.

Posterior midline to edge of scapula.

Inner canthus

Outer canthus

Supraclavicular fossa

Axilla (armpit)

Elbow crease

Wrist crease

Thenar eminence

Knee crease

12 cun

9 cun

12 cun

8 cun

8 cun

5 cun

19 cun

16 cun

20 cun

15 cun

3 cun

58 Key Points

These tables list the locations and main actions of 58 points, many of which are used in part three. Practise locating the points on your own, or your partner's body, using the techniques and anatomical information on pages 44–7. The points' actions range from the specific to the more general. For example, some points stop pain – they have an anaesthetic property; others have wider, tonifying functions.

Lung meridian

	Location	Main Actions and Uses
Lu 7 *Lie que* **Broken sequence**	1.5 cun above wrist crease, between abductor pollicis longus and brachioradialis, above styloid process.	Descends and disperses lung Qi. Circulates defensive wei qi; releases exterior; clears nose.
Lu 11 *Shao shang* **Lesser metal**	Radial side of end segment of the thumb. 0.1 cun from corner of thumb nail.	Expels wind; clears heat; descends and disperses lung Qi. Treats sore throat.

Large intestine meridian

	Location	Main Actions and Uses
LI 4 *He gu* **Joining valley**	Back of hand, between thumb and first finger, halfway down 2nd metacarpal, at bulge of muscle.	Expels wind; releases exterior; clears the channel; stops pain; influences the face. CONTRAINDICATED IN PREGNANCY (PROMOTES DELIVERY)
LI 10 *Shou san li* **Arm 3 miles**	On radial side of dorsal surface of forearm. 2 cun below LI 11 on elbow crease.	Removes obstructions from the channel; tonifies Qi. Treats muscular problems affecting forearm and hand.
LI 11 *Quchi* **Crooked pond**	Lateral end of cubital crease, at midpoint between lateral epicondyle of humerus and cord-like tendon of biceps.	Expels exterior wind; clears heat; cools blood; resolves damp; benefits tendons and joints.

Stomach meridian

	Location	Main Actions and Uses
St 8 *Tou wei* **Head corner**	0.5 cun above anterior hairline at corner of forehead. 4.5 cun lateral to midline of head.	Expels wind; relieves dizziness; relieves pain; clears head; benefits the eyes.
St 25 *Tian shu* **Heavenly pillar**	2 cun lateral to centre of navel.	Promotes functions of intestines. Treats retention of food, abdominal pain, diarrhoea and constipation. CONTRAINDICATED DURING PREGNANCY
St 28 *Shui dao* **Waterway**	3 cun below navel and 2 cun lateral to anterior midline.	Stops pain; benefits urination; regulates menstruation. CONTRAINDICATED IN PREGNANCY

	Location	Main Actions and Uses
St 29 *Gui lai* Returning	4 cun below navel and 2 cun lateral to anterior midline.	Relieves stagnation of blood. Treats menstrual problems. CONTRAINDICATED DURING PREGNANCY
St 36 *Zu san li* Leg 3 miles	3 cun below depression on outer side of knee. 1 cun lateral to crest of tibia.	Treats any digestive problems. Dispels cold; strengthens body; tonifies Qi, blood and Yin.
St 40 *Feng long* Abundant prosperity	8 cun above tip of external malleolus and 2 cun lateral to crest of tibia.	Resolves phlegm and damp; calms asthma; clears heat; calms and clears mind.
St 44 *Neiting* Inner courtyard	Junction of red and white skin, proximal to web between 2nd and 3rd toes.	Clears heat; eliminates fullness in stomach; stops pain; promotes digestion.
St 45 *Li dui* Sick mouth	Lateral side of end segment of 2nd toe. 0.1 cun from corner of toenail.	Calms mind; clears heat; relieves retention of food; brightens eyes.

Spleen meridian

Sp 1 *Yin bai* Hidden white	Medial side of end segment of big toe, 0.1 cun from corner of toenail.	Strengthens spleen; stops bleeding; calms mind.
Sp 3 *Tai bai* Greater white	Medial side of foot, in depression at junction of red and white skin, posterior and inferior to 1st metatarsophalangeal joint.	Strengthens spleen; resolves damp; strengthens spine.
Sp 4 *Gongsun* Grandfather and grandson	Medial side of foot at junction of red and white skin, below base of 1st metatarsal bone.	Tonifies stomach and spleen; regulates menstruation; calms spirit. Treats acute epigastric or abdominal pain.
Sp 6 *San yin jiao* Three yin meeting	3 cun directly above tip of medial malleolus, on posterior border of tibia.	Strengthens spleen; resolves damp; nourishes blood and Yin; benefits urination; moves blood; regulates menstruation; calms mind. CONTRAINDICATED IN PREGNANCY
Sp 8 *Di ji* Earth movement	3 cun below Sp 9, on a line connecting it to the tip of the medial malleolus. 5 cun below medial end of knee crease.	Removes obstructions from the channel; regulates uterus. Treats acute period pain.
Sp 9 *Yin ling quan* Yin mound spring	In depression posterior and inferior to medial condyle of tibia, on anterior border of gastrocnemius muscle.	Resolves damp; benefits lower burner; benefits urination; removes obstructions from the channel.
Sp 10 *Xue hai* Sea of blood	With knee flexed, 2 cun above medial corner of patella, on bulge of quadriceps.	Cools and tonifies blood; removes blood stasis; regulates menstruation. CONTRAINDICATED IN PREGNANCY
Sp 15 *Da heng* Great horizontal	4 cun lateral to the centre of the umbilicus.	Strengthens spleen and limbs; resolves damp; promotes functions of large intestine. Treats diarrhoea or constipation. CONTRAINDICATED IN PREGNANCY

Heart meridian

	Location	Main Actions and Uses
Ht 3 *Shaohai* Lesser sea	Midpoint between medial end of cubital crease and medial epicondyle of humerus.	Removes obstructions from the channel; calms mind; clears heart fire.
Ht 7 *Shen men* Spirit gate	At ulnar end of wrist crease, in depression on radial side of flexor carpi ulnaris tendon.	Calms mind; nourishes heart blood; tonifies heart Qi and heart yin.

Small intestine meridian

SI 3 *Hou xi* Back stream	In depression by 5th metacarpophalangeal joint, at junction of red and white skin.	Clears wind from spine and neck; expels exterior wind; benefits sinews; resolves damp; clears mind.

Bladder meridian *Points Bl 13 to Bl 25 are known as the 'Back transporting points'.*

Bl 13 *Fei shu* Lung point	1.5 cun lateral to lower border of spinous process of 3rd thoracic vertebra.	Treats all lung patterns. Regulates and tonifies lung Qi; stops coughing; clears heat; regulates nutritive and defensive Qi.
Bl 15 *Xin shu* Heart point	1.5 cun lateral to lower border of spinous process of 5th thoracic vertebra.	Treats any heart patterns. Calms mind; clears heat; invigorates blood; nourishes heart.
Bl 17 *Geshu* Diaphragm point	1.5 cun lateral to lower border of spinous process of 7th thoracic vertebra.	Nourishes and invigorates blood; opens chest; tonifies Qi and blood; calms mind.
Bl 18 *Ganshu* Liver point	1.5 cun lateral to lower border of spinous process of 9th thoracic vertebra.	Benefits liver and gall bladder; resolves damp heat; moves stagnant Qi; benefits eyes; eliminates wind.
Bl 20 *Pishu* Spleen point	1.5 cun lateral to lower border of spinous process of 11th thoracic vertebra.	Tonifies spleen and stomach; resolves damp; nourishes blood.
Bl 21 *Weishu* Stomach point	1.5 cun lateral to lower border of spinous process of 12th thoracic vertebra.	Major point to tonify stomach and spleen. Resolves damp; relieves retention of food.
Bl 22 *San jiao shu* Triple burner point	1.5 cun lateral lower border of spinous process of 1st lumbar vertebra.	Resolves damp; opens water passages; regulates transformation of fluids in lower burner.
Bl 23 *Shenshu* Kidney point	1.5 cun lateral to lower border of spinous process of 2nd lumbar vertebra.	Tonifies kidneys; strengthens lower back; nourishes blood; resolves damp; brightens eyes; benefits bones and hearing.
Bl 25 *Dachangshu* Large intestine point	1.5 cun lateral to lower border of spinous process of 4th lumbar vertebra.	Promotes functions of large intestine; strengthens lower back; clears channel; relieves fullness and swelling.

	Location	Main Actions and Uses
Bl 36 Cheng fu Receiving support	Middle of the transverse gluteal crease.	Soothes sinews. Treats lower back ache and sciatica.
Bl 40 Weizhong Bend middle	Centre of popliteal crease, between tendons of biceps femoris and semitendinosus.	Treats acute back ache by moving blood and clearing the channel. Clears heat; resolves damp; relaxes sinews.
Bl 60 kunlun Kunlun mountains	In depression between tip of external malleolus and Achilles tendon.	Expels wind; removes obstructions from the channel; relaxes sinews; clears heat; moves blood; strengthens back.

Kidney meridian

K 3 Tai xi Greater stream	In depression between tip of medial malleolus and Achilles tendon.	Tonifies kidneys; benefits essence; strengthens lower back and knees; regulates uterus.

Pericardium meridian

P 6 Nei guan Inner gate	2 cun above anterior wrist crease, between palmaris longus and flexor carpi radialis.	Opens chest; regulates heart Qi and blood; regulates and clears triple burner; calms mind; harmonizes stomach.

Triple burner meridian

TB 5 Waiguan Outer gate	2 cun above to dorsal wrist crease, between radius and ulna.	Releases exterior; removes obstructions from the channel; benefits hearing; subdues liver Yang.
TB 6 Zhigou Branching ditch	3 cun above to dorsal wrist crease, between radius and ulna.	Regulates Qi; removes obstructions from the channel; clears heat; expels wind; moves stagnant liver Qi.

Gall bladder meridian

GB 20 Feng chi Wind pond	Below occipital bone on neck, in depression between sternocleidomastoid and trapezius.	Eliminates wind; brightens eyes; benefits ears; clears heat; clears brain; subdues liver Yang. Treats headaches.
GB 21 Jian jing Shoulder well	On the highest point of shoulder, halfway between 7th cervical vertebra and acromion.	Descends Qi; relaxes sinews. Treats neck and shoulder problems. CONTRAINDICATED DURING PREGNANCY
GB 30 Huantiao Jumping circle	One third of the way from greater trochanter to sacral hiatus. (Locate by lying on side.)	Clears channel; tonifies Qi and blood; resolves damp heat. Treats lower back and hip problems and sciatica.
GB 34 Yang ling quan Yang hill spring	Lateral side of leg, in depression anterior and inferior to head of fibula.	Promotes smooth flow of liver Qi; resolves damp heat; removes obstructions from the channel; relaxes sinews.

	Location	Main Actions and Uses
GB 40 Qiuxu Ancestral mound	Anterior and inferior to lateral malleolus, in depression behind extensor digitorum longus.	Promotes smooth flow of liver Qi.

Liver meridian

	Location	Main Actions and Uses
Liv 3 Tai chong Supreme surge	In depression distal to junction of 1st and 2nd metatarsal bones.	Treats any liver pattern. Subdues liver yang; promotes smooth flow of liver Qi; calms mind.
Liv 8 Ququan Crooked spring	With knee bent, posterior to medial condyle of tibia and superior to border of tendons attaching at medial side of knee.	Benefits bladder; resolves damp in lower burner; relaxes sinews; nourishes liver blood; tonifies liver Yin; regulates liver Qi.
Liv 13 Zhangmen Chapter gate	Below free end of 11th floating rib.	Promotes smooth flow of liver Qi; relieves retention of food; benefits stomach and spleen.

Conception vessel meridian

	Location	Main Actions and Uses
CV 4 Guanyuan Origin gate	On anterior midline, 3 cun below navel.	Nourishes blood and yin; regulates uterus; tonifies kidneys; calms mind. CONTRAINDICATED DURING PREGNANCY
CV 6 Qi hai Sea of Qi	On anterior midline, 1.5 cun below navel.	Tonifies Qi and yang; regulates Qi; resolves damp. CONTRAINDICATED IN PREGNANCY
CV 12 Zhongwan Centre of epigastrium	On anterior midline, 4 cun above navel.	Tonifies stomach and spleen; resolves damp anywhere in body; regulates stomach Qi. Treats any digestive problems.
CV 13 Shangwan Upper epigastrium	On anterior midline, 5 cun above navel.	Subdues rebellious stomach Qi; calms mind; regulates heart.

Governing vessel meridian

	Location	Main Actions and Uses
GV 4 Mingmen Gate of line	Below spinous process of 2nd lumbar vertebra.	Tonifies kidney yang; nourishes original Qi; expels cold; strengthens lower back; benefits essence.
GV 14 Dazhui Great hammer	Between spinous processes of 7th cervical vertebra and 1st thoracic vertebra.	Clears heat; releases exterior; expels wind; regulates nutritive and defensive Qi; clears and calms mind; tonifies yang.
GV 20 Bai hui One hundred meetings	On top of head, midway between apexes of ears, and 7 cun above posterior hairline.	Calms mind; lifts spirits; tonifies yang; strengthens spleen's ascending function.

Extra points not found on the channels

	Location	Actions	
Yintang *Seal hall*	Midway between medial ends of eyebrows.	Eliminates wind; calms mind.	
Taiyang *Greater yang*	In depression about 1 cun posterior to lateral end of eyebrow and outer canthus.	Eliminates wind; clears heat; clears head; brightens eyes.	
Tunzhong	Half way between midline and edge of buttock, level with sacral hiatus.	Removes obstructions from the channel. Treats lower back pain and sciatica.	

Moving on ...

You have now reached the end of the first part of this book, covering the principles of traditional Chinese medicine. You have been introduced to the language of Chinese medicine and to all the main building blocks of theory that form the basis for understanding disease in terms of this unique medical system. As you move on to the Tui Na techniques in part two, it is vital that you keep in mind all that you have learned so far.

To recap, disease is an expression of an underlying disharmony in the balance of a person's Yin and Yang energies. Yin and Yang are then further divided into the eight guiding principles. These help you, as the practitioner, to identify patterns of disharmony in terms of excess and deficiency, hot and cold, interior and exterior and Yin and Yang. Combine these principles with an understanding of the functions and relationships of the vital substances and internal organs, and you will be able to work out any pattern of disharmony from any list of signs and symptoms. The theory of the five elements provides you with another angle on diagnosis and on the holistic nature of human beings.

Although you now know enough bare bones to work out patterns of disharmony and to formulate a basic diagnosis, I must emphasize that it takes years of study to gain a thorough understanding of this subject. If you are serious about getting to grips with it, I recommend the text books listed in Resources *(see page 139)*.

To improve your ability to identify patterns of disharmony, take case histories from as many of your friends as possible. Follow the four examinations *(see pages 30–35)* and gather as much information as you can, keeping the following questions in mind:

- What organ or organs are affected?
- Is the pattern of disharmony interior or exterior? Hot or cold? Excess or deficient? Yin or Yang?
- Are there any pathogenic factors present?
- What is the state of the individual's Qi and blood?
- What are the possible causes of this disharmony?

Look at lots of tongues. Have a go at feeling pulses and generally observe the people you meet on a daily basis. In part two we will move away from the brain work to the manual work of techniques and learning several Qi Gong exercises.

The Techniques

You have now been introduced to the theory that forms the foundation of all branches of traditional Chinese medicine – Tui Na, acupuncture, Chinese herbal medicine and Qi Gong. In this section of the book, you will learn how to practise twenty of the most commonly used Tui Na techniques, so that you can apply them to treat common ailments, as shown in part three.

It can be difficult to learn physical movements and techniques from a book, so, to make things as clear as possible, there are instructions and photographs throughout, plus useful tips to make sure you keep on track. Every technique has its own particular therapeutic effects on the body. For example, Tui fa (pushing technique) can be used to relieve pain and warm the meridians. To keep you in mind of this, you will find a description for each technique of its actions in terms of Chinese medicine and some examples of the ailments it is applied to in treatment.

Practising Tui Na can be physically demanding. Some of the techniques require continuous repetition for up to 20 minutes. To help you build your physical and energetic strength and stamina, I have included several Qi Gong exercises in this section, the majority of which come from the Shaolin Qi Gong system. This form of Qi Gong is a powerful and dynamic one, taught to Tui Na students at the beginning of their training to strengthen their muscles and bones and to develop their Qi (see pages 17–18). I can remember being taught Shaolin Qi Gong in China – after the first 4 intense days, I started dreaming about bending metal bars with my bare hands.

Two of the techniques in this section are difficult to master and require a lot of practice to get right. They are Gun fa (rolling) and Yi zhi chan tui fa (one-finger meditation). They are always taught first for three main reasons: they strengthen the muscles, tendons and joints in the hands and arms; the other techniques come easily once these two are mastered; and they are constantly used in practice for their renowned therapeutic effects. If you practise these two techniques and the Qi Gong exercises every day for 3 months, you will give yourself a very strong grounding on which to build up your proficiency and effectiveness in applying Tui Na.

What You Will Need

Equipment

Fortunately very little equipment is needed in the practice of Tui Na. A massage table is the best place to give a treatment. Chairs without arms and stools are also used when treating areas such as the neck and shoulders. If you do not have a massage table, it is possible to practise most techniques with your partner lying on the floor, preferably on a futon or several blankets. However, this does become uncomfortable for the practitioner, as you cannot use your body posture as effectively as you can when standing.

You will need a rice bag to practise the two most difficult techniques: Gun fa (rolling) and Yi zhi chan tui fa (one-finger meditation). Make the bag out of material such as strong cotton. It should be about 30 cm (12 in) long by 15 cm (6 in) wide and 10 cm (4 in) deep. Fill it with rice so that it is quite firmly packed. There is a story that the old Chinese Tui Na teachers would give their students a rice bag after showing them how to practise Gun fa and Yi zhi chan tui fa, and tell them to return when they had ground the rice down to powder through their practice. Only then were they ready to work on a human body.

Unless a massage ointment is being used, Tui Na is generally applied through clothes. It is common in China to wrap a cloth over the patient's clothes on the area to be worked on. This provides a smooth surface to work on. However, I find working over a T-shirt and tracksuit bottoms, or the equivalent, is ideal.

Massage media

Massage media are often applied to the skin as part of a treatment. They can be applied to points or to local areas where the techniques will be used. Generally, they act as lubricants, but specific preparations are also used to treat particular ailments. For example, ginger juice can be used to disperse cold, release the exterior and warm the stomach and spleen. This can be useful in treating colds, vomiting, abdominal pain and wryneck. Strong alcohol is sometimes used, such as whisky, brandy or rice wine, to activate circulation of Qi and blood, resolve damp, ease pain, soften the sinews and strengthen bones. It can be used pure or as a base for soaking Chinese herbs. Plain cold water is commonly used to clear fever in children. Some of the most useful media are listed below. All the ingredients are easy to get hold of from Chinese supermarkets. *(See Further reading, page 139, for more information on preparations.)*

Toasted sesame oil

Toasted sesame oil is very useful, and I use it frequently on the abdomen and back. It is slightly warming and is beneficial in treating spleen Qi deficiency which may be causing diarrhoea, tiredness and lack of appetite.

Talcum powder

This is useful if you wish to work directly on the skin, as it will reduce friction and protect the patient's skin and the skin on your hands.

Dong qing gao

This is useful for many musculoskeletal problems and is often used when applying the technique Ca fa.

Ingredients and method

  250 g/½ lb Vaseline (petroleum jelly) or vegetable fat
  6 g/¼ oz menthol crystals
  1 tablespoon wintergreen oil

Melt the Vaseline or fat in a pan. Remove from heat. Add menthol crystals and wintergreen oil. Mix and pour into suitable containers while still liquid. Allow to cool.

Ginger and spring onion tincture

This is used to treat the common cold and to disperse cold from the epigastric and abdominal areas.

Ingredients and method

  30 g/1 oz fresh ginger
  30 g/1 oz spring onion bulbs
  250 ml/8 fl oz white alcohol (vodka, maotai or white rum)

Soak the ginger and spring onion in alcohol for 2 weeks. Strain and store. This is great for treating children. If you are short of time, just simmer the ginger and spring onion in water for 15 minutes. Allow to cool.

Qi Gong

The practice of Tui Na is physically and energetically demanding. It requires strength, stamina, flexibility and sensitivity. In order to achieve these qualities, it is essential to practise Qi Gong exercises. They will also develop the strength of your Qi, or internal force, which – when combined with a Tui Na technique – increases the effectiveness of the treatment. Practising the Qi Gong exercises given in this book will be of great benefit to you personally as well as for developing your Tui Na techniques. They will strengthen your resistance to disease, improve your posture, increase your energy levels and vitality, improve your circulation, and give you great muscle tone. I would also encourage you to go to a Qi Gong class of your choice once a week.

General fitness

Alongside your Qi Gong, general daily exercise is very important. Yoga, swimming, walking, running – find what suits you. Meditation is also of immeasurable benefit. From a practitioner's point of view, it increases your ability to focus your mind and attention on what you are doing, to stay in the present moment in your body, in your centre, and to practise from a loving and generous heart. I also recommend the Alexander Technique, which I have personally found to be invaluable in helping me practise Tui Na consistently for several years. It teaches us how to use our bodies with the minimum amount of tension and the maximum efficiency.

Developing internal force

This exercise encourages Qi to build up in the Dan Tien, the area inside your belly. Practise this exercise once a day and follow it with 'The pulling of Qi' exercise overleaf. The more you practise, the easier it will become to keep your mind focused.

During the exercise, you may become hot and start to sweat. After a few weeks of practising on a regular basis, your body may start to move spontaneously: your legs may begin to shake and your body twitch of its own accord. Allow this to happen – it is a sign that your force is building up and moving through any blockages in your meridian system. Your breathing pattern may also change. Whatever occurs, do not fight it. Keep relaxed and go with your body's consciousness. Do not use any muscular effort – the strength required for the exercise comes from your mind.

Building up Qi

Stand in the position shown keeping as relaxed as possible. Bend your knees slightly and hinge forwards from the groin, as if you were about to sit on a high stool. Focus your attention on Pericardium 8. Imagine you are pushing these two points together very strongly. Push with your mind as hard as you can. Keep pushing for 5–10 minutes.

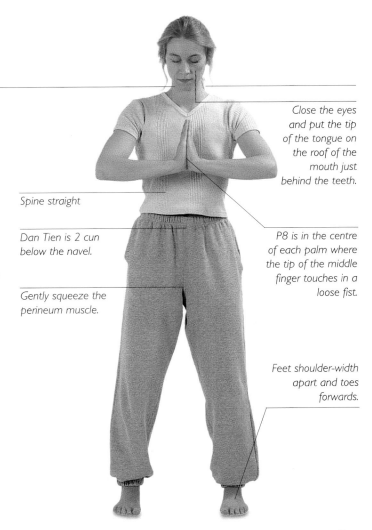

Close the eyes and put the tip of the tongue on the roof of the mouth just behind the teeth.

Spine straight

Dan Tien is 2 cun below the navel.

Gently squeeze the perineum muscle.

P8 is in the centre of each palm where the tip of the middle finger touches in a loose fist.

Feet shoulder-width apart and toes forwards.

The pulling of Qi

Practise this every day to help develop Qi and direct it to your hands for Tui Na. Keep your body relaxed. If you like, shift your body weight from foot to foot and pull the elastic in different directions.

Palms hollow.

Spine straight.

Palms flat.

Knees slightly bent.

Step one ▷
Bring your palms together at your navel with fingers pointing forwards. Imagine that points P8 on each hand are connected by a strong piece of elastic. Stretch the elastic outwards as far as you can.

◁ Step two
Imagine the elastic contracting, pulling your palms towards each other. Continue like this for 5–10 minutes.

Step three
Level to your navel, imagine you are holding a (football-sized) ball of Qi between your palms. Close your eyes and feel any sensations in and around your palms. Remain like this for 3–5 minutes, then relax.

Clearing exercise

I practise this between patients and at the end of the day. It clears any stagnation which may have built up in the meridians and increases the circulation of Qi and blood.

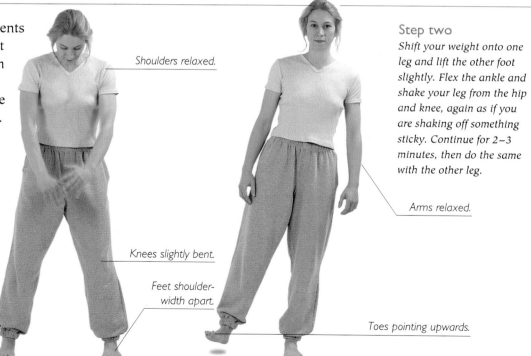

Shoulders relaxed.

Knees slightly bent.

Feet shoulder-width apart.

Arms relaxed.

Toes pointing upwards.

Step one
Bring your weight slightly forwards and bend from your groin as if you were about to sit on a high stool. Let your arms hang loosely in front of you. Cross your left hand over your right so they are close but not touching. Shake both hands deliberately and forcefully, as if you were trying to shake off something sticky. Continue for 2–3 minutes.

Step two
Shift your weight onto one leg and lift the other foot slightly. Flex the ankle and shake your leg from the hip and knee, again as if you are shaking off something sticky. Continue for 2–3 minutes, then do the same with the other leg.

Standing for health

This exercise, also known as 'Holding a ball of Qi', has several functions: it develops Qi and promotes its circulation throughout the meridian system; it promotes and maintains health; it grounds and centres the body and Qi; it increases mental focus; it calms the mind and emotions; and it develops sensitivity to what Qi feels like.

To begin with, practise for just 5 minutes each day for 2 weeks. Then increase to 10 minutes for a further 2 weeks; then to 15 minutes. Try to practise at the same time each day. Find a time that works for you, when you will not be disturbed. The best place to practise is outside in nature (especially near a big tree). But the most important thing is that the place feels calm and good to you.

Keep as relaxed as possible throughout the exercise. Your hips, shoulders, jaw and neck are the most likely places for unconscious tension to collect. If your mind wanders, gently bring your attention back to your hands and to your breathing. Imagine a cord running from your coccyx at the base of your spine, all the way up your spine, up the back of your head to your crown.

Breathe gently through your nose.

CV 12 is midway between the navel and sternum.

Place the tip of the tongue on the roof of the mouth just behind the teeth.

Breathe into your Dan Tien, below the navel.

Gently pull up the perineum muscle.

Knees slightly bent.

Toes forwards.

Step one
Stand with your feet shoulder-width apart. Think about someone pulling the imaginary cord from your crown; imagine a puppeteer suspending a puppet from a string. Tell your whole body to relax on the outside and the inside. Hang your arms loosely at your sides.

Step two
Imagine a string attached to the back of each of your wrists and that someone is pulling the strings and lifting your wrists to the level of CV 12. Keep your hands relaxed and your shoulders and elbows dropped throughout.

Step three
Turn your wrists, palm up, with fingertips facing each other but not quite touching. Keep your elbows out: imagine a balloon under each armpit. Close your eyes and concentrate on your palms. Imagine you are holding a paper ball and be aware of sensations in your palms.

Shaolin Qi Gong standing positions

The exercises that follow are from the Shaolin system. They can be practised in the four standing positions shown here. For the best results, vary the positions you use. The standing positions can be practised on their own without adding the exercise movements. They will, in themselves, strengthen your muscles, tendons and bones, develop your stamina, and build up your Qi.

Shaolin Qi Gong is dynamic and powerful. You will get hot and probably sweat doing these exercises. If you are practising the standing positions on their own, hold the position for about 3 minutes to start with, then relax and walk around for a few minutes before coming back to repeat it. Build your time up gradually by 1 or 2 minutes per week until you reach 10 minutes.

Position one

Stand with your feet quite close together and turn your toes in until your big toes are touching. Pull up and tense your leg muscles and buttocks and grip the floor with your toes. Pull both arms back, pushing up with the heels of your palms. Make sure your arms are completely straight, and tense the muscles. Keep your fingers straight and together and your thumbs extended.

Position two

Stand with your feet shoulder-width apart, your feet parallel and toes pointing forwards. Pull up and tense all the muscles in your legs and buttocks as hard as you can. Grip the floor firmly with your toes. Your arms are exactly the same as for position one.

Position three

Stand with your feet about twice your shoulder-width apart, your toes turned slightly inwards and your knees bent. Grip the floor with your toes and tense the muscles of your legs and buttocks. Your arms are exactly the same as described in position one.

Position four

Stand with your feet together, then, keeping your hips straight, take a giant step forwards with one foot into a lunge position. Bend your front leg until your knee is in line with your toes. Turn your back foot slightly outwards. Practise this position on both sides to ensure even development.

The phoenix spreads its wings

Practise this Shaolin Qi Gong exercise to help you master Rou fa *(kneading technique, see pages 70–71)*. When you have completed the movement, relax, stretch and walk around. Then repeat it 3–6 times, always relaxing in between. Begin from one of the four standing positions *(see opposite)*. Breathe naturally through your nose throughout, keeping your leg muscles tense and your toes gripping the floor.

Step one △
From the standing position, bring your attention to the L shape formed by your index fingers and thumbs. Imagine pushing a great force forwards and upwards with this part of the hands until you arrive just in front of your armpits, with your elbows tucked into your sides. Keep your fingers and thumbs rigid.

Step two ▷
Keeping the muscles of your hands and arms tense, push them forwards from the L shape, as if pushing away a great force. Keeping the tension at all times, gradually cross your hands over at the wrists. Your elbows should be slightly bent.

Step three △
Now, bring your attention to your little fingers and the outer edge of your palm. Push a force outwards to the sides. Keep your muscles tense – they may begin to shake at this point – and continue until your arms are fully extended to the sides.

Step four
Bringing your attention back to the L shape of your thumbs and index fingers, push the great force back in until your wrists are crossed over as before. With your muscles still tensed, pull your arms backwards to the original starting position and hold this for about 2 minutes.

Pushing eight horses forwards

Practise this Shaolin Qi Gong exercise to help you master Ca fa *(scrubbing technique, see pages 76–7)*. You should find a great improvement in your technique after practising. Begin from one of the four standing positions *(see page 60)*. Keep the muscles of your legs as tight as possible throughout and your toes gripping the floor, then relax, walk around and stretch. Repeat the exercise 3 times in total, relaxing in between.

◁ Step one
From your standing position, focus your attention on the L shape formed by your thumbs and index fingers. Imagine you are pushing a great force forwards and up until your hands reach to just below your armpits. Your palms should be facing your ribs, with the heels of your palms touching your ribs, your fingers held tightly together, your thumbs sticking up and your elbows tucked into your sides.

Step two ▽
Now begin to push your arms forwards. Imagine you are pushing the weight of eight horses forwards with your fingers and thumbs. Your arms may begin to shake with the muscular effort required. When your arms are fully extended, pause in this position briefly, keeping all your muscles tense.

Step three
Now, using the strength of your shoulders and arms, begin to pull the eight horses backwards until your hands return to just below your armpits. Keeping your arms and hands tense, push a great force down and backwards until you are back in your original standing position. Hold this for 2–3 minutes.

Pushing a boat forwards

Practise this Shaolin Qi Gong exercise to help you master Zhen fa *(vibrating technique, see pages 84–5)*. Stand in one of the four standing positions *(see page 60)*. Throughout the movement, keep your leg muscles pulled up and tense and grasp the floor with your toes. After completing the exercise, stretch, relax and walk around. Repeat the exercise 3 times in total, relaxing in between.

Step one
From your standing position, focus on the L shape formed by your thumbs and index fingers and imagine you are pushing a great force forwards and up until your hands reach to just below your armpits. The heels of your palms should touch your ribs, with your thumbs sticking up and your elbows tucked in. Now, keeping the muscles of your arms and hands tense, turn your palms inwards until they face the wall opposite you.

Step two
Bring your attention to the palms of your hands. Imagine your hands are on the back of a huge boat and begin to push the boat forwards. Think of the strength it would take to do this. Keep your arm muscles tight. Your arms and hands may begin to shake. Keep pushing until your arms are fully extended. Pause in this position for 1–2 minutes.

Step three
Turn your hands and pull them back with as much strength as you pushed forwards, until they are tucked by your armpits again. Push a great force down and back until you are in your original position. Hold for 2–3 minutes.

Pulling the golden ring with one hand

Practise this Shaolin Qi Gong exercise to help you master Dou fa *(shaking technique, see page 85)*. Begin in one of the four standing positions *(see page 60)*. Throughout the exercise keep the muscles in your legs pulled up and tight and grasp the floor with your toes. When you have finished, release all your muscles. Walk around and stretch a little, then repeat the exercise 3 times in total, relaxing between each time.

Step one

From your standing position, bring your attention to the L shape formed by your thumbs and index fingers. Imagine pushing a great force forwards and up until your hands reach the area just below your armpits. The heels of your palms are touching your ribs, your thumbs sticking up and your elbows tucked in.

Step three ▽

Continue pushing until your arm is fully extended. Now visualize a huge ring made of solid gold hanging down in front of you. Begin to turn your hand so that your thumb is pointing downwards and your palm is turned away from you. As you do so, make a fist around the ring.

Step four ▽

Imagine you have taken hold of this golden ring. Turn your fist so that the palm side of your hand is facing inwards again. Now pull the ring back towards you until you reach just in front of your armpit. It should be a great effort. Release your fist and return to the L-shaped hand position.

Step two △

Once you have brought your hands to below your armpits, bring your attention to the fingers and thumb of your left hand. Begin to push your hand and arm forwards as if you were pushing something huge and heavy away with your fingers and thumb.

Step five

Now pull the golden ring with your right hand, leaving your left hand where it is. Then pull your arms and hands down and backwards, as if against a great force, until you are back in the original standing position. Hold this for 2–3 minutes.

Lifting up the cauldron

Practise this Shaolin Qi Gong exercise to improve your An rou fa *(revolving technique, see page 89)*. Begin from one of the four standing positions *(see page 60)* and keep your leg muscles tense and your toes gripping the floor throughout. After completing the movement, release your muscles, stretch a little and walk around. Repeat the exercise 3 times in total, relaxing between each sequence.

Step one
From your standing position, concentrate your attention on the L shape formed by your thumbs and index fingers and imagine you are pushing a great force forwards and up until your hands reach just below your armpits, with your elbows tucked in, your fingers together with your thumbs sticking up.

Step five
Turn your hands, at the wrists, until the palms are facing each other with the fingers pointing to the sky. Form the L shape between your thumbs and fingers again. Imagine you are holding the cauldron between your hands.

Step two △
Keeping your arms and hands tense, turn your wrists, pushing up with the heels of your palms until your fingers are pointing out to the sides. Your palms should now be turned upwards to the sky.

Step three △
Imagine holding a cast-iron cauldron. Push it up until you reach just above your head. Then turn your hands until your fingertips are facing each other and continue pushing up.

Step four △
Continue to lift up the huge, heavy cauldron. It should be a real effort and your arms may begin to shake. When your arms are fully extended, with elbows straight, hold this for 1 minute.

Step six △
Pull the cauldron down until you arrive back at your armpits. Then return your hands to the starting position by pushing down and backwards. Hold the standing position for 2–3 minutes.

Gun Fa *rolling*

撥
法

Gun fa is one of the hardest techniques to master and takes a lot of practice to get right. When done correctly, it looks very easy and relaxed. This is one of the techniques that must be practised on your rice bag before attempting to apply it to your partner. It took me about 3 months of daily practice to really get to grips with Gun fa on my rice bag, and a further 6 months to become competent on a human body. It is worth persevering though, as it is one of the most commonly used techniques in practice and is renowned for its therapeutic effects.

Gun fa has a deep, penetrating and warming effect and is generally applied to large muscle groups. The best places to start practising are the back and the top of the shoulders (the trapezius). Gun fa is usually the first technique applied for musculoskeletal ailments to relax the recipient and to soften and warm the muscles. When the technique becomes second nature to you and is flowing effortlessly, you can be very specific with it and focus on small areas, even individual points.

The sequence shown below constitutes one rolling cycle. Repeat this over and over again. Remember that the rolling movement does not start in your hand. Your elbow and the extensor muscles of your forearm propel and power the movement. Your little-finger knuckle should be a focus point; imagine it is glued to one point and cannot be moved. It also helps to think of your arm as a wing moving gracefully and smoothly at all times and your hand as a greasy metal ball.

Practising Gun fa

Initially, practise for 10–15 minutes each day. After 2 days of practising with your dominant hand, introduce your other hand to the movement. From then on, practise for an equal amount of time with both hands – it is important to learn to do Gun fa with both hands. Build your practice up to 20–25 minutes per day and, after 6–8 weeks, your hands and arms will be far more flexible and your muscles stronger. If you feel ready at this point, you may start practising on your partner.

Step one
Begin with the little-finger edge of your hand on the bag with your palm and fingers naturally flexed. Then, by extending your wrist, roll onto the back of your hand.

Step two
Keep rolling until your palm is open and facing upwards with your fingers and wrist fully extended. Then roll your hand back to the starting position.

Rice-bag work

Place your rice bag on a table and position the little-finger side of your hand on the bag. Now roll the back of your hand onto the bag. A triangular area between the head of your ulna and your third and fifth knuckles should be in contact with the bag. When your wrist is fully extended and your elbow and forearm are away from the side of your body, press firmly onto the rice bag with the back of your hand.

Immediately and smoothly roll back to the starting position. Your elbow and forearm should move in towards the side of your body. As you practise, you will be able to build up your speed and pressure.

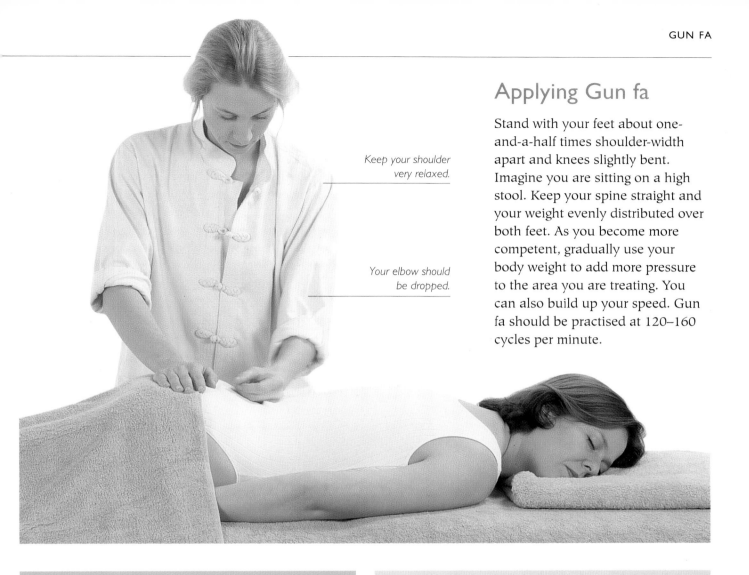

Keep your shoulder very relaxed.

Your elbow should be dropped.

Applying Gun fa

Stand with your feet about one-and-a-half times shoulder-width apart and knees slightly bent. Imagine you are sitting on a high stool. Keep your spine straight and your weight evenly distributed over both feet. As you become more competent, gradually use your body weight to add more pressure to the area you are treating. You can also build up your speed. Gun fa should be practised at 120–160 cycles per minute.

Tips for practice

- Be as smooth and rounded as you can. There should be no jerky movements.
- Observed from behind, the movement of your elbow and arm should look like a wing flying in and out.
- Be consistent in pressure and speed. You can start gently and moderately if working on a painful area, gradually building up speed to between 120–160 cycles per minute.
- Your fifth-finger knuckle should stay in contact with the area being treated at all times.
- Gun fa can be used progressively along an area or meridian.
- Relax, keep breathing and watch your posture: keep upright and avoid hunching.
- Gun fa can be used with both hands working simultaneously.

Where on the body? Apply to the back, buttocks, legs, arms, shoulders and abdomen. It can be used to stimulate points, but is mainly used on large muscle groups.

What are the effects? Relaxes the tendons and muscles, warms and clears meridians, expels wind cold and damp, increases the circulation of Qi and blood and removes stagnation and stasis, relieves swelling, lubricates joints, relieves pain.

What can it treat? Injuries of soft tissues, Bi Syndrome, lower back problems, sciatica, spasm and contraction of tendons and muscles, abdominal pain, abdominal fullness and bloating, frozen shoulder, neck problems, numbness of muscles.

Yi Zhi Chan Tui Fa *one-finger meditation*

一指禪推法

As with the previous technique, Gun fa, Yi zhi chan tui fa is difficult to master and needs a lot of practice on the rice bag before being applied to the human body. This is another essential technique for a Tui Na practitioner to acquire. It is used time and time again as it is the main technique for stimulating points along the meridians. Yi zhi chan tui fa is the Tui Na practitioner's equivalent of the acupuncturist's needle. A clue to the technique is in its name. 'Chan' means meditation, which suggests prolonged focus and attention in a relaxed manner.

Stimulation of points

To strengthen or tonify a point, use the technique more gently, and propel the movement in the direction of the natural flow of Qi in the meridian concerned (*refer to Meridians, pages 36–43*). Also, visualize Qi coming from the universe, through you, to the tip of your thumb and penetrating the point, giving Qi to where it is needed.

To clear or reduce a point, apply strong stimulation by making the technique powerful and vigorous. Propel the movement against the natural flow of Qi in the meridian concerned. (Note that in the sequence shown below, movement is directed towards the left.) Always keep the treatment principle in your mind and imagination.

Practising Yi zhi chan tui fa

It is important to learn to do Yi zhi chan tui fa with both thumbs. Start by practising for 2–3 minutes a day with each thumb and gradually increase by 2–3 minutes each week until you reach 20–25 minutes' practice per day. It can feel particularly awkward and uncomfortable when you first start, but after a few months of regular practice it begins to come naturally. Once you have mastered Yi zhi chan tui fa and Gun fa, the other techniques will feel very easy by comparison.

Step one
With your thumb fixed to the spot, use the muscles of your forearm to propel your wrist and relaxed fingers away from your body, extending your thumb fully.

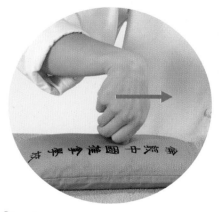

Step two
Contract your forearm muscles to roll your wrist back towards your body, bringing your fingers in towards your thumb, which now flexes backwards slightly.

Rice-bag work

Sit with your rice bag in front of you on a table and both feet flat on the floor, about shoulder-width apart. Mark a spot on your bag – this represents a point to be stimulated.

Place either the tip or pad of your thumb on the mark. Whether you

use the tip or pad depends on your personal anatomy – if the end joint in your thumb is very flexible, you will find it easier to use the pad; most people, however, use the tip.

Keeping your thumb fixed to the marked point, use the power of your forearm to propel your wrist away

from your body, extending your thumb. Then bring your wrist back towards you, flexing your thumb backwards a little. This completes one cycle. Repeat this over and over again to get the flow and rhythm of the movement. As you practise, build up your speed.

Applying Yi zhi chan tui fa

Begin to practise slowly for the first few weeks and, as you become more familiar and confident with the technique, start to build up your speed. In practice, this technique should be done at 120–160 cycles per minute. As you become more proficient, add more pressure by using the weight of your arm.

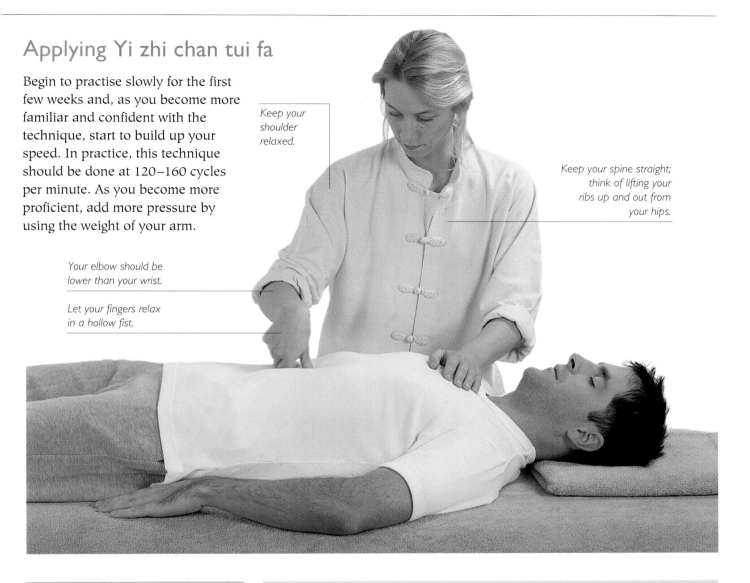

Keep your shoulder relaxed.

Keep your spine straight; think of lifting your ribs up and out from your hips.

Your elbow should be lower than your wrist.

Let your fingers relax in a hollow fist.

Tips for practice

- Keep your thumb glued to the point at all times. Do not let it wander around off course.
- Make sure your shoulder is relaxed. Do not let it creep up towards your ear.
- Imagine your arm is resting on a tennis ball in your armpit.
- Keep relaxed and get into a rhythm with the movement.
- Focus your mental attention and your energy on the tip of your thumb.

Where on the body? Apply to any points and meridians on the body.

What are the effects? Activates points and therefore the particular actions of the points – for example, it activates circulation of Qi and blood, disperses stagnation, strengthens stomach and spleen. To strengthen or tonify a point, move in the direction of the flow of Qi along its meridian. To reduce or clear a point, move against the direction of the flow of Qi.

What can it treat? Headaches, insomnia, dizziness, hypertension, abdominal and epigastric pain, period pains, traumatic injuries. It is used for both internal and external ailments.

Rou Fa *kneading*

揉
法

Rou fa is a commonly used Tui Na technique and can be applied to many parts of the body. You may be relieved to know that it is an easy technique to acquire, especially in comparison to the previous two. There is no need to practise Rou fa on your rice bag, but I would advise you to first practise on yourself just to get the feel of it – try your thigh or forearm.

You can apply Rou fa with your thumb, your middle finger, your fingers and thumb together, your whole palm, the heel of your palm or the tip of your elbow.

The three methods described below are the most common. If you want to use another method, follow the same principles of downward pressure and circular kneading. Try the exercise 'The phoenix spreads its wings' *(see page 61)* to help improve your technique.

Stimulation of points

Rou fa with your thumb or middle finger can be used to stimulate points. To strengthen or tonify a point, use gentle clockwise kneading. To clear or reduce a point, use anticlockwise kneading and more pressure.

Using thumb

Sit or stand with your spine straight. If you are standing up, have your feet one-and-a-half times shoulder-width apart and knees bent. This gives a solid base from which to work and helps protect your back.

Select a point or area to work on. Put your thumb on the area and bend the end joint backwards slightly so that you are using the pad of your thumb rather than the tip. Apply some strength and pressure downwards with your body weight, then begin to knead the underlying muscles round and round. Start slowly and gently and, as the area softens and warms, increase the speed of the technique until you are doing 100–160 circles per minute.

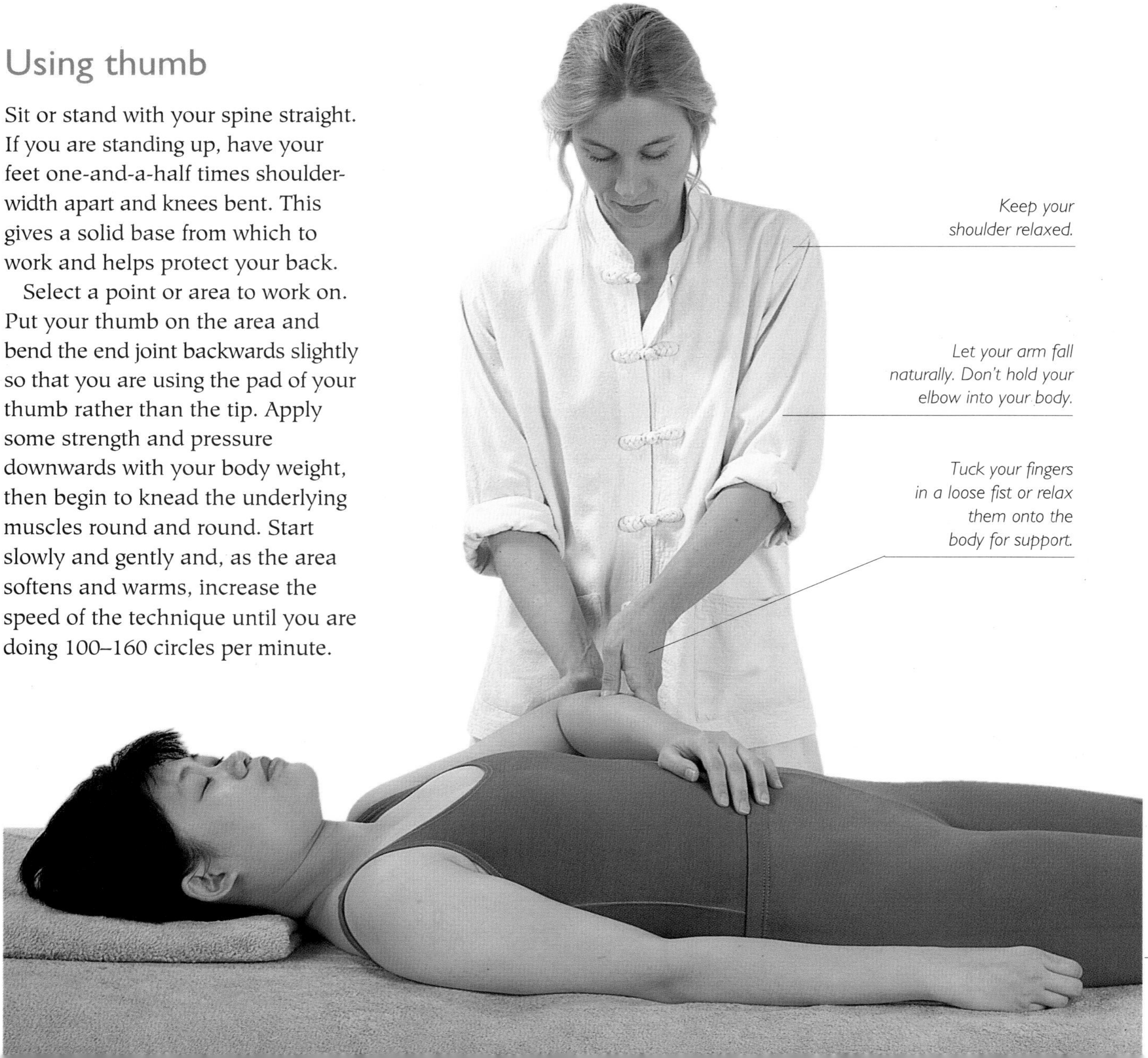

Keep your shoulder relaxed.

Let your arm fall naturally. Don't hold your elbow into your body.

Tuck your fingers in a loose fist or relax them onto the body for support.

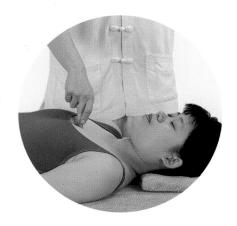

Using middle finger

Place the pad of your middle finger on a selected point or area and put your index finger over the top. Attach your thumb to the back of the end joint of your middle finger to give extra support to the technique. The end segment of your middle finger should be bent slightly back. Apply a little pressure downwards onto the point by relaxing your shoulder and arm and making use of your arm's natural weight. Knead the underlying muscles in a continuous circular motion. Begin slowly and gently, gradually building up speed and pressure as the point or area being worked on begins to warm up.

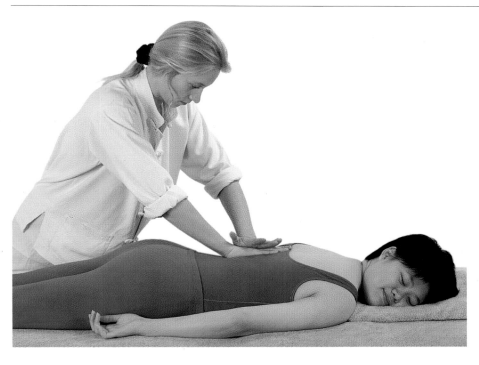

Using heel of palm

This form of Rou fa is generally done standing up, and is best practised on your partner's back or limbs. Place the heel of your palm on the area to be treated and relax your fingers down onto your partner's body. Keep your shoulder relaxed and apply strength and pressure downwards through your wrist using your body weight. Keeping the heel of your palm fixed to the area, knead the underlying muscles in generous circles.

Tips for practice

- Always move the underlying muscles and do not skim over the surface of the skin.
- Rou fa should feel deep and penetrating but also pliable and soft.
- You can move the technique from one place to another. For example, over a whole muscle group or along the course of a meridian.
- Start slowly and gently, gradually increasing your pressure and speed.

Where on the body? Thumb and finger kneading is mainly used on points. The heel of the palm or whole palm is used on the back, legs, arms, abdomen and buttocks. The elbow is used mainly on the buttocks.

What are the effects? Activates points, invigorates flow of Qi and blood, reduces swelling, relieves spasm, stops pain, calms mind, clears meridians, opens chest, relaxes muscles, strengthens stomach and spleen.

What can it treat? Headaches, dizziness, insomnia, constipation, diarrhoea, epigastric pain, muscular pain, numbness, stiffness and spasm, soft tissue injuries, sprains.

Mo Fa *round rubbing*

Mo fa is a simple Tui Na technique that is quite easy to learn and you can begin to practise it on your partner straight away. It feels very relaxing and comforting to receive.

Mo fa is generally applied using a single palm. However, in the case of certain digestive ailments, particularly when an underlying deficiency of Qi is the root cause, Mo fa is applied on the belly with the palms joined.

This technique is most commonly used on the belly and the head. When applied to the head, it is known as stroking and caressing the head.

Try practising the 'Clearing exercise' *(see page 58)* to help you master this technique.

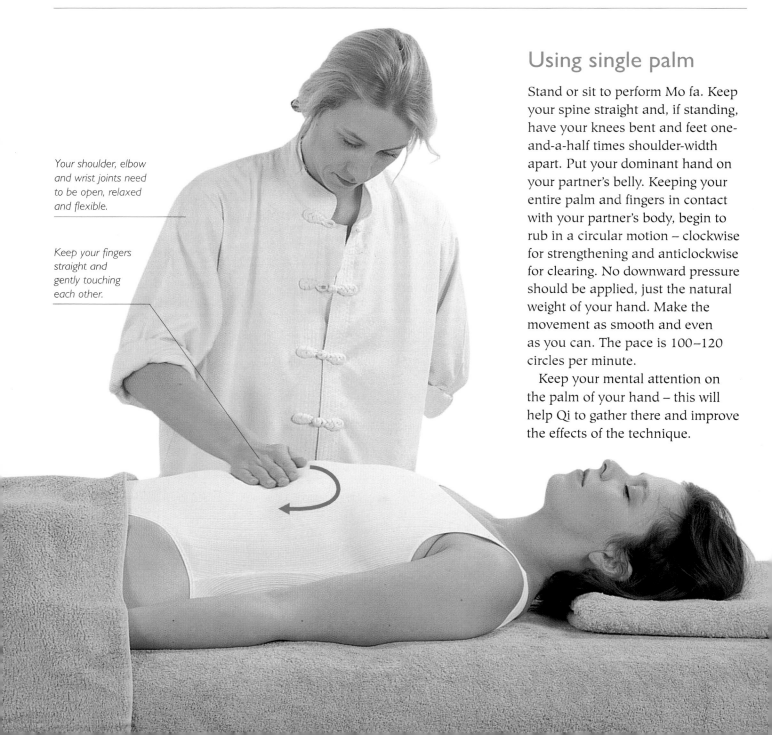

Your shoulder, elbow and wrist joints need to be open, relaxed and flexible.

Keep your fingers straight and gently touching each other.

Using single palm

Stand or sit to perform Mo fa. Keep your spine straight and, if standing, have your knees bent and feet one-and-a-half times shoulder-width apart. Put your dominant hand on your partner's belly. Keeping your entire palm and fingers in contact with your partner's body, begin to rub in a circular motion – clockwise for strengthening and anticlockwise for clearing. No downward pressure should be applied, just the natural weight of your hand. Make the movement as smooth and even as you can. The pace is 100–120 circles per minute.

Keep your mental attention on the palm of your hand – this will help Qi to gather there and improve the effects of the technique.

Using joined palms

Sit or stand, as described opposite. Form an L shape between your index fingers and thumbs by extending your thumbs, then overlap one hand on top of the other by interlocking the two L shapes. Put your joined palms onto your partner's belly, keep your shoulders, elbows and wrists open and relaxed, and begin to rub in a circular movement as you did when using a single palm.

This form of Mo fa is useful for strengthening and tonifying and is applied in a clockwise direction on the belly.

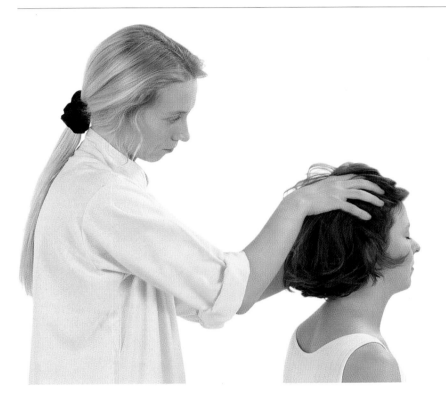

Using palm and fingers

With your partner seated, stand either in front of or behind her. Starting from the left side of the forehead, use your dominant hand to round rub with your palm and finger pads, gently and softly at first. Work from the forehead over the left side of the head to the back of the left side of the head. Then from the centre of the forehead over the crown and down the middle of the back of the head. Then do exactly the same on the right side. Repeat the round rubbing, gradually increasing the speed of the technique until the head feels very warm.

Tips for practice

- Be as relaxed and fluid as possible.
- Get into a rhythm with the movement.
- Keep your attention on your palm and fingers.
- Think of polishing something very precious.

Where on the body? Apply to the chest, ribs, epigastric area, abdomen and head.

What are the effects? Moves stagnant liver Qi, warms the middle burner, strengthens spleen, regulates stomach, improves digestion, regulates intestines, removes food stagnation, disperses cold, relieves swelling. Use clockwise round rubbing for strengthening, and anticlockwise for clearing.

What can it treat? Headaches, insomnia, constipation, diarrhoea, abdominal pain, epigastric pain, stress.

Na Fa *grasping*

Na fa is a very satisfying technique to apply and is quite easy to master. You can practise on yourself or your partner straight away. On yourself, try working on the muscles of your arms or thighs.

Na fa can be applied in three ways: with the pads of your thumb, index and middle finger; with the pads of your thumb and all four fingers; or with your whole hand. You may like to try incorporating a little Rou fa *(see pages 70–71)* with this technique.

Applying Na fa

Na fa is generally performed from a standing position. Give yourself a solid base to work from by standing with your feet one-and-a-half times shoulder-width apart and your knees slightly bent. Grasp the selected tendon or muscle in one of the ways shown below. Grip and squeeze it between your thumb and fingers, then lift it

up away from the underlying bones. Now release the muscle and repeat for several minutes on the area being treated. Na fa should be rhythmic and firm but not rough or hard. Begin slowly and gently and gradually increase the pace and strength applied as the area being worked on warms up.

With one hand
Attach the pads of your thumb and all four fingers (shown here on the neck). Or, use just your thumb and index and middle fingers.

With two hands
Try adding a twisting jerking movement by pulling your hands briskly in opposite directions back and forth several times.

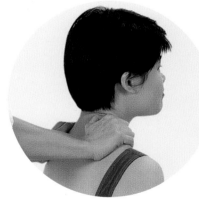

With whole hand
Attach your palm and your fingers and thumb to a selected muscle and grip, as described above.

Tips for practice

- Use the pads of your fingers, not your fingertips, and avoid digging your nails into the skin.
- You can use both hands together.
- Keep an even rhythm.
- Think about warming and softening the area you are working on.

Where on the body? Apply to the head and the muscles and tendons of the neck, shoulders, arms, legs, back and abdomen.

What are the effects? Relaxes muscles and tendons, relieves muscle spasm and pain, expels wind and cold, promotes circulation of Qi and blood, clears meridians, improves eyesight.

What can it treat? Common cold, stiff neck, dizziness, low back pain, sprains.

Cuo Fa *rub rolling*

搓
法

Cuo fa is a technique used generally at the end of a treatment to relax the patient and to stimulate and regulate the flow of Qi and blood throughout an entire area. For example, if you are working on someone's shoulder joint, you would apply Cuo fa starting from the top of the joint and gradually working your way down the whole arm. Cuo fa is not difficult, but it is quite strenuous and requires the even coordination and strength of both hands.

Working on the arm

To work on your partner's arm, have him seated and stand at the side of the arm with your feet one-and-a-half times shoulder-width apart, knees bent and back straight.

Put one hand on either side of his shoulder, with your fingers pointing upwards. Hold the joint loosely between your hands then lift it up using the heels of your palms. Now begin to rub and roll the shoulder between your hands quite rapidly. Maintaining the rub rolling movement, start to move smoothly and slowly down your partner's arm all the way to his hand. Repeat 3 times in total, keeping the frequency and pressure even.

Working on the flanks

Ask your partner to sit on a stool, and stand behind him in a low posture, as with the previous method. Put one hand either side of the ribcage, just below his armpits. Hold the ribcage between your hands and rub roll rapidly. Slowly and smoothly work your way down to the bottom ribs. Do this 3 times.

Tips for practice

- Keep in a low posture.
- Move down the area slowly, rub rolling rapidly.
- The movement should not be too large – keep it neat.
- Move the underlying muscles. Do not skim the surface of the skin.
- Rub roll firmly. Imagine towelling someone dry who is freezing cold.

Where on the body? Apply to the ribcage, shoulders, arms and legs.

What are the effects? Relaxes tendons and muscles, regulates Qi and blood flow, clears meridian obstructions.

What can it treat? Asthma, breathing problems, flank pain, shoulder and elbow problems, muscle tension.

Ca Fa *scrubbing*

擦
法

Ca fa is one Tui Na technique that must be applied directly to bare skin using some form of lubricant. Dong qing gao ointment *(see page 56)* is a popular massage media for Ca fa, especially in the treatment of musculoskeletal problems. Pure talcum powder can also be used to help resolve damp; and toasted sesame oil to strengthen the spleen and muscles.

Ca fa is a dynamic technique requiring strong shoulder muscles, and is difficult to get just right. Done correctly, it produces incredible heat, making the skin scorching hot. Practise the exercise 'Pushing eight horses forwards' *(see page 62)* to improve your technique.

You can apply Ca fa using the whole palm, the heel of the palm, the thenar eminence or the little-finger edge of the palm, depending on the area you are treating.

Using whole palm

Ca fa is performed from a standing position. Keep in a low posture with your knees bent and your feet one-and-a-half times shoulder-width apart. Put your hand on the area being treated. Now, drive your hand forwards then back. Keep your hand in contact with the skin surface at all times. The movement should be as large as you can make it.

The strength and force is in the forwards and backwards movement. There should be no downward pressure at all as this will prevent the production of the desired heat. The rate of Ca fa is about 100 cycles per minute, but you need only do 10 cycles to any one area. Any more than this and the skin becomes too hot and you could create blistering or scalding.

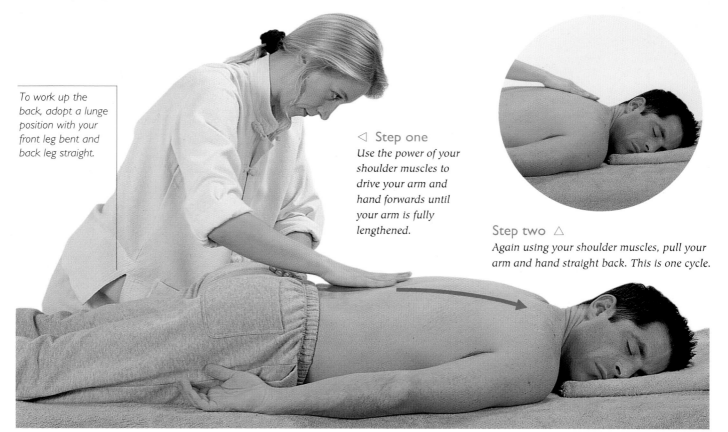

To work up the back, adopt a lunge position with your front leg bent and back leg straight.

◁ **Step one**
Use the power of your shoulder muscles to drive your arm and hand forwards until your arm is fully lengthened.

Step two △
Again using your shoulder muscles, pull your arm and hand straight back. This is one cycle.

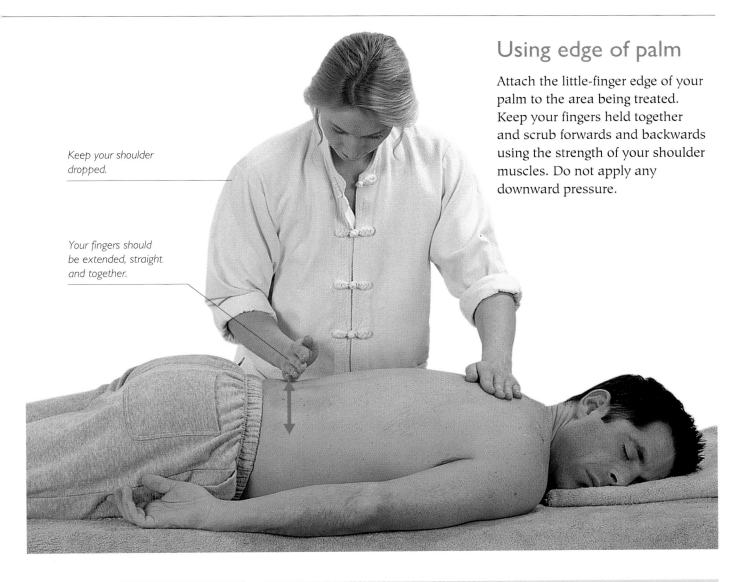

Keep your shoulder dropped.

Your fingers should be extended, straight and together.

Using edge of palm

Attach the little-finger edge of your palm to the area being treated. Keep your fingers held together and scrub forwards and backwards using the strength of your shoulder muscles. Do not apply any downward pressure.

Tips for practice

- Think of polishing a huge wooden table.
- Keep your hand in contact with the skin at all times.
- Make the backwards and forwards movement big and straight.
- Do not press downwards, even slightly.
- Let the force come from your shoulder.

Where on the body? Apply to the back, chest, abdomen, arms and legs. Your whole hand is best used for large areas, such as the back, chest and abdomen. Your palm heel or thenar eminence (fleshy mound at base of the thumb) are used for the legs and arms. The little-finger edge of your palm for the sacrum and lower back.

What are the effects? Warms meridians, removes obstructions from meridians, activates circulation of Qi and blood, reduces swelling, stops pain, opens chest, expels wind and cold, strengthens stomach and spleen.

What can it treat? Lower back ache and sciatica, musculoskeletal problems, deficiency of Qi and blood, deficient conditions of the internal organs.

An Fa *pressing*

An fa is probably the oldest Tui Na technique. It is relaxing and comforting, both to receive and to give, but requires sensitivity, awareness and mental focus – the exercise 'Standing for health' *(see page 59)* will help with this.

The thumb is used to stimulate most points. Knuckles provide stronger stimulation. The tip of the middle finger is useful for points on the belly and rib area. The palm or heel of the palm is used for larger areas (the back, buttocks, legs and belly).

Using thumb

Place the pad of your thumb on the point to be stimulated. Keep your shoulder relaxed and apply pressure with your body weight, not the strength of your arm. Start lightly and gradually increase the pressure. Your hand may become warm or numb; this is a sign that you have activated the point. Be sensitive to your partner's body. If she feels an aching sensation, you have reached the depth required and the point is being stimulated. Continue for 5–10 minutes, applying constant pressure or releasing and reapplying it intermittently and rhythmically. Apply An fa in the same way with your middle finger or knuckles.

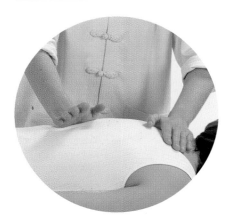

Using heel of palm

With your partner lying down, place the heel of your palm (or your whole palm) on the area to be treated. Keep your arm straight and wrist bent. Lean your body weight onto your partner. Once you have reached the desired pressure, pause for anything up to 5 minutes, if your partner's Qi is deficient. If you want to move stagnant Qi and blood, you need only pause briefly before releasing the pressure. Keep the heel of your palm (or your palm) in contact with your partner and slide it along the muscle slightly, then reapply. Continue in this manner along the area being treated several times.

Tips for practice

- You can sit or stand to apply An fa.
- Use your weight, not your strength.
- Be aware of any sensations. If your partner's muscles resist, pull back.
- Enjoy the technique. The more relaxed you are the better.

Where on the body? Apply to any points along the meridians and to the back, buttocks, belly, chest, arms, legs and head.

What are the effects? Calms the mind, dispels anxiety, relaxes and strengthens muscles and tendons, relieves pain and spasm, clears meridians, regulates Qi flow, moves blood, adjusts joints, regulates functions of the internal organs.

What can it treat? Insomnia, headaches, abdominal pain, stuffiness of the chest, epigastric pain, general muscular aches and pains.

Ya Fa *suppressing*

Ya fa is a stronger, more intense, version of An fa. It is applied with the tip of the elbow, the forearm and, on occasion, the knees. It is used where very strong stimulation is required on large muscular areas or points that are very deep, such as GB 30 on the buttocks. I use the tip of the elbow here as an example because it is by far the most commonly used form of Ya fa in Tui Na.

Applying Ya fa

Stand with your feet shoulder-width apart and knees bent. Place the tip of your elbow on the area to be treated. Now lean your body weight into the muscles, gently at first, slowly increasing the pressure by leaning your body more. The sensation felt by your partner should be quite a strong ache. Pause for 3–5 minutes then gradually release the pressure.

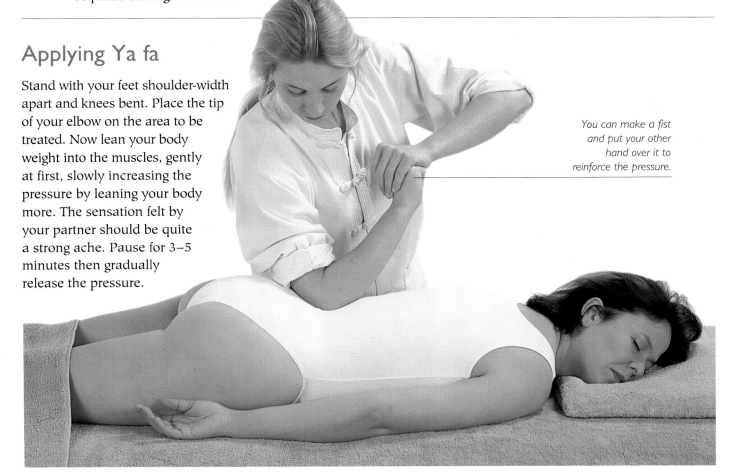

You can make a fist and put your other hand over it to reinforce the pressure.

Tips for practice

- Don't be frightened of leaning your body weight onto your partner. It will only hurt if you hold back and tense up.
- Lean in slowly and smoothly.

Where on the body? Apply to the buttocks, backs of the legs and back (where the muscles are thick).

What are the effects? Activates flow of Qi and blood, removes obstructions from the meridians, relaxes spasm, relieves pain, expels cold and wind, moves stagnant Qi and blood.

What can it treat? Sciatica, lower back ache, dizziness, liver and stomach disharmony.

Tui Fa *pushing*

推法 Tui fa is a simple technique that you can use on your partner straight away. It involves pushing in a straight line from one place to another, often along part of a meridian. It can be applied over clothing or directly to the skin using a lubricant, such as talcum powder *(see page 56)*. Tui fa is most commonly applied with the thumb, the heel of the palm or both palms. It can also be done with one palm, the fist or the tip of the elbow. In adults, thumb pushing is mainly used on the head and neck.

Applying Tui fa

Tui fa is generally performed standing with feet shoulder-width apart and knees slightly bent. Place your hand on the area to be treated and apply a little downwards pressure using the weight of your arm. Push a straight line forwards, then immediately pull backwards along the same line. This completes one cycle. The forward pushing should be reasonably strong and penetrating and the backwards movement soft and gentle.

With thumb
Put the radial (outer) edge of your thumb pad onto the area being treated. Tuck your fingers into your palm or rest them on the body.

With heel of palm
Put the heel of your palm on the area to be treated. Extend your wrist and your fingers; fingers can be closed or slightly separated.

With both palms
Put both of your palms on the area to be treated. Have your thumbs touching and your fingers quite close together.

Tips for practice

- For all methods of Tui fa the speed is about 100 cycles per minute.
- The forwards pushing should be quite strong and warming and the backwards movement gentle, light and soft.
- Make Tui fa rhythmic, consistent and smooth.

Where on the body? Thumb pushing is used on the face, head, neck and nape. The heel of the palm is used on the chest, belly, back, arms and legs. Both palms are used on the back, belly and ribs.

What are the effects? Clears head, opens chest, warms and clears meridians, aids digestion, moves stagnant Qi, promotes circulation of Qi in the chest, strengthens stomach and spleen, relaxes muscles, relieves pain.

What can it treat? Headaches, dizziness, coughs, asthma, chest pain, digestive problems, stiff neck, muscular spasm, lower back ache.

Ma Fa *wiping*

Ma fa, like Tui fa, is one of the easier techniques to acquire. It is a gentle technique used mainly on the face, head and neck and is applied using the pad of the thumb or the pads of both thumbs simultaneously.

Ma fa is a relatively small, but fast, wiping movement which is applied in lines either vertically or horizontally on the body. It is a very pleasant technique to receive and has a calming, soothing effect on the patient.

Applying Ma fa

Ma fa is usually performed in a standing position but is also possible to do seated. Choose whichever is most comfortable for you, but remember to keep your spine straight and your shoulders relaxed. Place the pad of your thumb or the pads of both thumbs on the area to be treated and gently wipe up and down or from side to side in straight lines. The wiping should be a small, controlled and relaxed movement. No pressure is required. Be gentle, but not hesitant – imagine you are wiping off a dirty mark from the skin. The speed of this technique should be 100–120 cycles per minute.

With one thumb
Using the pad of your thumb, wipe back and forth horizontally from the spine out over the muscles at the back of the neck, then back in towards the spine.

With two thumbs
Begin with your thumbs together at the centre of your partner's forehead and wipe outwards to the area just above the ends of the eyebrows then back to the centre. Continue wiping in lines all the way up the forehead to the hair line and then down again.

Tips for practice

- Keep your spine straight and your shoulders relaxed.
- Be gentle, even and rhythmic.
- Do not be too superficial with Ma fa. Avoid floating on the surface of the skin.
- You may apply some lubricant, such as talcum powder, if you wish, especially if your partner's skin is quite dry.

Where on the body? Apply to the face, head, neck and nape.

What are the effects? Calms the mind, improves eyesight, soothes pain, relaxes the muscles and tendons, aids circulation of Qi and blood.

What can it treat? Headaches, dizziness, stiff neck, short sightedness.

Ji Fa *chopping*

Ji fa is one of my favourite Tui Na techniques. It can be applied in several different ways, some of which are more physically exerting than others. Chopping with the edge of the palms is quite demanding and requires some stamina to keep it going. Striking with a hollow fist using the back of your hand is far less strenuous, as is striking or dotting using your fingertips. Some people find Ji fa quite easy to acquire while others find it rather more tricky. I would advise you to practise for a few days on your rice bag or on your own thigh before using the technique on someone else.

Using palm edge

This is commonly used on the back, top of the shoulders, arms and legs. Stand with your feet one-and-a-half times shoulder-width apart and your knees bent in a low, stable posture. When working on the shoulders and upper back, alter your height by bending your knees. Keeping your fingers and hands relaxed, chop the little-finger edge of your palm against the area to be treated.

The movement comes from your elbow and wrists, so the more elastic and loose they are the better. If you stiffen up, the technique will become painful to the receiver. This method of Ji fa is dynamic, but should feel comfortable and pleasant to receive. Begin slowly and gently, gradually building up force and speed until it is as fast as possible, keeping it even and rhythmic throughout.

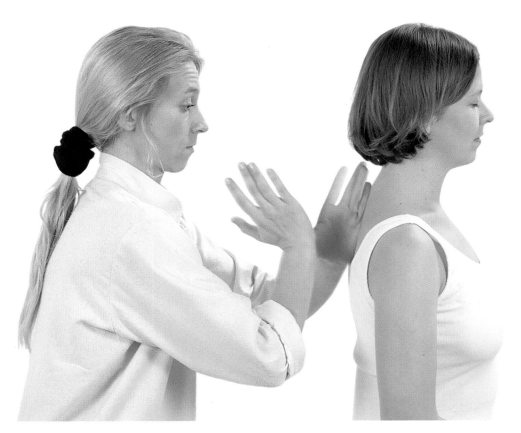

◁ **With separate palms**
'Bounce' your hands against your partner's body – imagine they are a pair of drumsticks. Relax and get into a rhythm. Try putting on some music with a strong beat and chop in time to it.

With joined palms △
Join your palms together, cross your thumbs over each other, and extend your fingers, keeping them slightly separated. Keep your elbows and wrists loose and relaxed. It should sound like slapping down a wet fish!

Using back of the hand

This method of Ji fa is used mainly on the back. Place the back of your dominant hand on your partner's back and curl your fingers and thumb in a loose, hollow fist. Keep your shoulder relaxed and your wrist straight throughout. Moving from the elbow, lift your hand up, and then relax your elbow so that the hand drops down again onto the back. Repeat, keeping relaxed.

Start slowly and build up to a moderate speed. Do not use any force: it should feel like your hand is bouncing off the muscles.

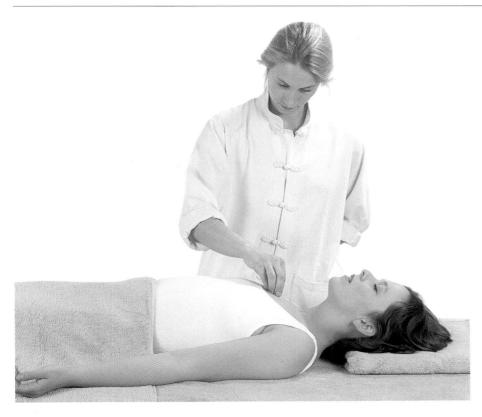

Using fingertips

Also known as dotting, this is used mainly on the head, abdomen, chest, legs and arms. Gather your thumb and fingers together so they are touching at the ends (in a shape like a bird's beak). Now relax your shoulder, drop your elbow, and put your fingertips on the area being treated. A relaxed, flexible wrist is essential, as the action is mainly from here. Lift your hand, then strike your fingertips down and bounce back up off the body. Repeat this, building up to a moderate speed, keeping a steady rhythm.

Tips for practice

- Rhythm is the key to this technique.
- Whichever method you are using, your hands should feel as if they are bouncing off the body.
- Relax. Remember to enjoy the technique and not to tense up.

Where on the body? Apply to the back, buttocks, arms, legs, abdomen, chest, head and shoulders.

What are the effects? Opens chest, resolves phlegm, relaxes tendons and muscles, stimulates flow of Qi and blood, clears meridians, clears stagnation, eases pain.

What can it treat? Coughs, asthma, abdominal bloating, tiredness, muscular spasm, lower back ache, stiffness of back and shoulders.

Zhen Fa *vibrating*

振法

Zhen fa is difficult to master – it took me about 6 months. Practise on your rice bag for 2–3 weeks before working on someone. It demands strong arm muscles, mental focus and dynamic internal Qi. Qi Gong, in particular 'Developing internal force' and 'Pushing a boat forwards' *(see pages 57 and 63)*, will help.

Zhen fa requires you to transmit a high-frequency up-and-down vibration which penetrates deep into the body. It is relaxing and calming to experience.

Applying Zhen fa

Stand with feet shoulder-width apart, spine straight and knees slightly bent. Bring your attention to the area of your abdomen known as Dan Tien, corresponding to CV 6 (this is where your internal force resides). Imagine moving this force up through your body and down your arm. Place your finger or hand on the area being treated, mentally direct your Qi and tense your arm muscles (as in Shaolin exercises). Keeping your shoulder relaxed, vibrate your hand up and down. The area you are working on will become warm. Generally, you will need to sustain Zhen fa for 3–5 minutes, but practise in short bursts to start with – a little each day.

With finger: method one
Vibrate the pad of your middle finger, with your index finger over the top of it.

With finger: method two
Vibrate the tip of your middle finger with your index finger pressed to the side of it.

With palm
Vibrate with the centre of your palm on the area being treated.

Tips for practice

- Keep the muscles in your arm tense.
- Do not press downwards. Use the weight of your arm.
- Vibrate up and down, not sideways.
- Practise the Qi Gong exercises.
- Be patient – eventually the vibration will be strong and even.

Where on the body? Finger vibration is used on points. Palm vibration is used on the abdomen, ribs and chest.

What are the effects? Calms mind, clears brain, improves eyesight, warms middle burner, regulates Qi flow, promotes digestion, regulates intestines, opens chest, resolves retention of food, stimulates functions of points.

What can it treat? Insomnia, headaches, anxiety, vertigo, nausea, abdominal and epigastric pain, painful periods.

Dou Fa *shaking*

抖
法

Dou fa is an easy technique to acquire, so you will be able to put it into practice straight away. It is used only on the arms and legs – most frequently on the arms – and is often used with Cuo fa *(see page 75)* at the end of a treatment to relax the muscles and joints. It is very important to keep your back straight and elbows bent, and to use your body weight to create a little traction. Practise the exercise 'Pulling the golden ring' *(see page 64)* to improve your technique.

Working on the arm

Your partner may be lying down on her back or seated on a stool. Take her arm by the wrist with both hands – not too tightly – and lift it up and slightly out to the side. Stretch the arm to create a little traction, then shake it up and down with a small movement. The shaking should begin at a moderate speed and build up gradually until very rapid. Shake at least 20 times.

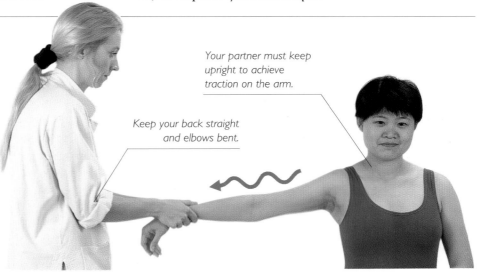

Your partner must keep upright to achieve traction on the arm.

Keep your back straight and elbows bent.

Working on the leg

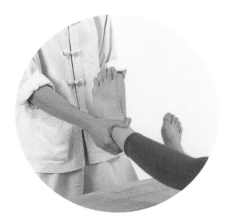

Your partner will need to be lying on her back on a massage table. Stand in a low squat with your back straight. Take hold of your partner's ankle with both hands and lift the leg up a little and out to the side slightly. Keep your elbows bent and shoulders relaxed; drop your body weight back so that you can stretch the leg, creating a little traction. Now begin to shake the leg up and down with a small movement. Start slowly and build up speed. You probably will not be able to shake the leg as fast as the arm because it is heavier. Shake at least 10 times.

Tips for practice

- Use your body weight to achieve traction.
- Keep the up-and-down movement relatively small.
- Start slowly and build up speed.
- Try interchanging Dou fa with Cuo fa (rub rolling).

Where on the body? Apply to the arms and legs.

What are the effects? Regulates Qi and blood flow, relaxes muscles and joints, removes obstructions from meridians.

What can it treat? Joint problems, musculoskeletal conditions, such as frozen shoulder and tennis elbow.

Yao Fa *rotating*

揺
法

Yao fa is a relatively simple Tui Na technique that involves the smooth rotation of any joint in the body, from the toes to the head. It is used in the treatment of musculoskeletal ailments to aid the joints and to relax the muscles and tendons. The technique is gradually introduced towards the end of a treatment after other techniques have been applied to warm up and relax the muscles and stimulate the flow of Qi and blood. Below and opposite are the most commonly used methods of applying Yao fa.

Some patients find it difficult to relax and give you the weight of their limb or head. Encourage them to breathe deeply and be firm and confident with your movements.

Working on the shoulder

Ask your partner to sit on a stool, and stand at the side of the shoulder you wish to rotate (rotation of the left shoulder is described here). Keep your feet about shoulder-width apart, your back straight and your knees slightly bent. Take hold of your partner's left wrist with your left hand and lift the arm up to the side until it is just below the level of the shoulder. Put your right hand on top of her shoulder joint. Now take a step forward with your left foot so you come into a lunge position. At the same time, begin to rotate your partner's arm by moving your left hand up and forwards. Now take a step back with your left foot to return to your starting place.

Continue rotating in this manner, stepping forwards and back, for about 10 rotations. You can move clockwise and anticlockwise – I usually do 5 in each direction. Mirror the technique when working on the other shoulder.

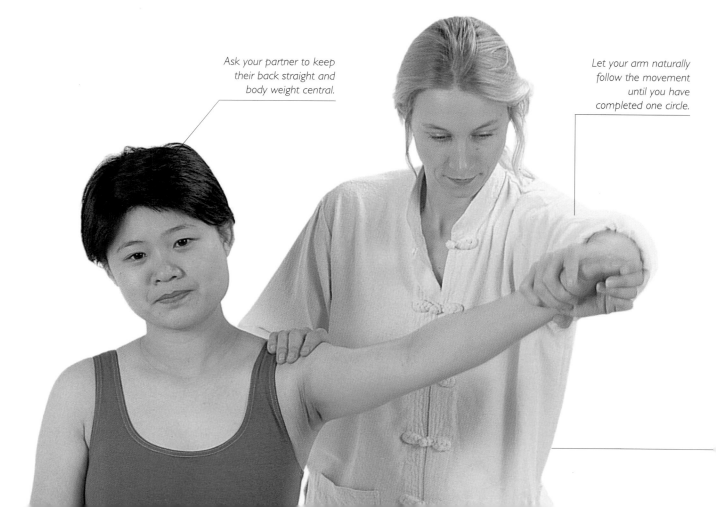

Ask your partner to keep their back straight and body weight central.

Let your arm naturally follow the movement until you have completed one circle.

Working on the neck

Once again, your partner should be seated with her back straight. Stand behind and slightly to one side of her and put one hand on her forehead and the other hand at the back of her head. Now begin to rotate the head in clockwise or anticlockwise circles. Imagine you are holding a football in your hands and are rolling it around between your palms. Start rotating in small circles and increase the size of the rotation gradually. The speed should be moderate at all times. Keep it smooth and rounded, avoiding any sudden jerky movements. Rotate the neck about 10 times.

Working on the hip

Ask your partner to lie on her back. If you are working on the right hip, stand to her right side. Take her right ankle with your right hand and put your left hand under the back of her knee. Bend the knee up towards your partner's chest. You can now either leave your right hand holding the ankle or you can cup the right heel in the palm of your right hand. Begin to rotate your partner's hip in a clockwise or anticlockwise direction. Start with small circles and, as the hip begins to release, increase the size of the movement until it is quite large. Rotate about 10 times.

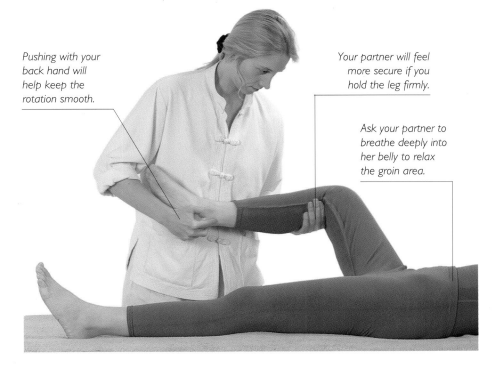

Pushing with your back hand will help keep the rotation smooth.

Your partner will feel more secure if you hold the leg firmly.

Ask your partner to breathe deeply into her belly to relax the groin area.

Tips for practice

- Rotate at a moderate speed, smoothly and evenly – do not make any jerky movements.
- Relax and be firm – but not rough – this will help your partner feel secure and prevent her or him tensing up.
- Coordinate your hands evenly.

Where on the body? Apply to any joints: such as, hips, shoulders, neck, wrists, ankles, fingers and toes.

What are the effects? Relaxes muscles and tendons, opens up joints, releases spasm, increases mobility.

What can it treat? Swelling and pain of joints, sprains, stiff neck, lower back ache, frozen shoulder.

Ban Shen Fa *pulling stretching*

Ban shen fa is mainly used for musculoskeletal ailments. It involves pulling and stretching the body to release muscle spasm and correct the position of the joints. The two methods of Ban shen fa shown below are very useful. Before applying it to the lumbar area, warm up the muscles with some Gun fa (rolling) and Rou fa (kneading).

Its sister technique, Ban fa (pulling), is also used to correct joint position, but I feel that Ban fa should only be learned under the supervision of a trained practitioner.

As a lumbar stretch

With your partner lying on his front, stand opposite the side you want to stretch; so, if you want to stretch the right lumbar area, stand to his left. Lift his left leg with your right hand under the knee cap and put your left hand just right of the spine on the lower lumbar muscles. The heel of your palm should be close to his spine but not on it. Now push down gradually with this hand, at the same time lifting the left leg higher until there is natural resistance. (If you wish, apply Rou fa with the heel of your left palm.) Hold the stretch for about 1 minute, release and gently lower the leg. Repeat on the other side.

As a neck stretch

Stand behind your seated partner with your feet shoulder-width apart and knees slightly bent. Your partner should be straight and relaxed with his limbs uncrossed. Form an L shape with both your index fingers and thumbs and hold your partner's head with both hands just below the base of his skull and lower jaw. Firmly, but not roughly, pull the head up gradually until there is a natural resistance. This creates space between the neck vertebrae. Hold for about 2 minutes, then release. Do this 2–3 times, then apply Na fa (*grasping technique, see page 74*) to the back of the neck.

Tips for practice

- Stretch gradually until you feel a natural resistance in the muscles.
- Ask your partner to breathe deeply.
- Keep relaxed; do not force the stretch.
- Avoid sudden movements.

Where on the body? Apply to the neck, shoulders, wrists, back, legs, fingers and toes.

What are the effects? Relaxes muscle spasm, relieves pain, lubricates joints and corrects position of joints, stimulates circulation of Qi and blood.

What can it treat? Lower back ache, sciatica, stiff neck, frozen shoulder and a variety of musculoskeletal problems.

An Rou Fa *revolving*

按
揉
法

An rou fa is a combination of pressing and kneading. It is a deeper, more penetrating technique than Rou fa (kneading) and is applied mainly with the muscles of the forearm and, occasionally, with the tip of the elbow.

An rou fa involves a fairly rapid circular revolving movement that stimulates the underlying muscles of various parts of the body. It is most frequently applied to the belly and lower back. It is pleasant and relieving to receive and is very satisfying to perform. There is no need to practise An rou fa on your rice bag – you can practise on your partner straight away. The best place to start is on the lower back.

Applying An rou fa

Ask your partner to lie face down. Stand to one side and place the ulna (little-finger) side of your forearm onto the area being treated. Now revolve the underlying muscles by rotating your forearm and moving it over the area. Work clockwise to tonify or strengthen, anticlockwise to clear or reduce. Keep going until you or your partner feel a sensation of warmth building up. It should feel deep but also soft. Do not let your arm float over the skin surface – as one of my teachers used to say, 'Move the muscles, not the skin.'

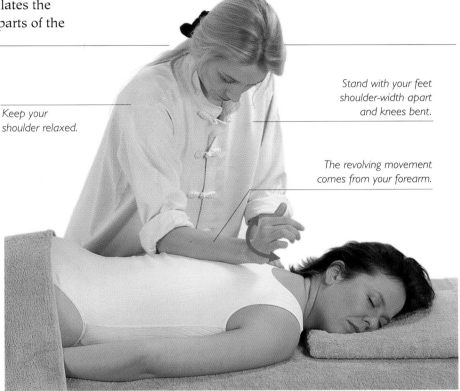

Keep your shoulder relaxed.

Stand with your feet shoulder-width apart and knees bent.

The revolving movement comes from your forearm.

Tips for practice

- Use the muscular part of your forearm.
- Keep the movement brisk, not slow.
- Do not move away from the area being stimulated.
- Work deeply but gently.
- Work to achieve a warm sensation.
- Move the underlying muscles, not the surface of the skin.

Where on the body? Apply to the back, belly, chest, buttocks and shoulders.

What are the effects? Moves stagnant Qi and blood, subdues liver, expels wind, clears heat, improves functions of intestines, improves digestion, relaxes muscles, relieves spasm, eases pain. Work in a clockwise direction to tonify or strengthen, anticlockwise to clear or reduce.

What can it treat? Epigastric and abdominal pain, painful periods, constipation, diarrhoea, lower back ache and sciatica.

Pia Fa *knocking*

拍
法

Pia fa is a simple Tui Na technique. It is applied with either a cupped palm or a hollow fist to various parts of the body and has several therapeutic effects. The cupped palm method is used mainly on the back. The hollow fist method can be applied in two ways, shown opposite. You can practise Pia fa on your partner straight away without any rice-bag practice. However, if you feel uncertain, this a good technique to practise on yourself. Your thigh muscles are perfect for this purpose.

There is no need to rush Pia fa; just take your time and pause between each knock.

Using cupped palm

With your partner lying face down, put the cupped palm of your dominant hand over the area being treated. Now lift your palm about 25 cm (10 inches) and let it fall with moderate force. Immediately let your hand bounce up again – this completes one knocking movement. Let your cupped palm hover for 2 seconds before repeating the knocking. Do not use lots of muscular strength. If you've got it right, your palm should make a hollow low sound. If you hear a high slapping sound, it's not quite right.

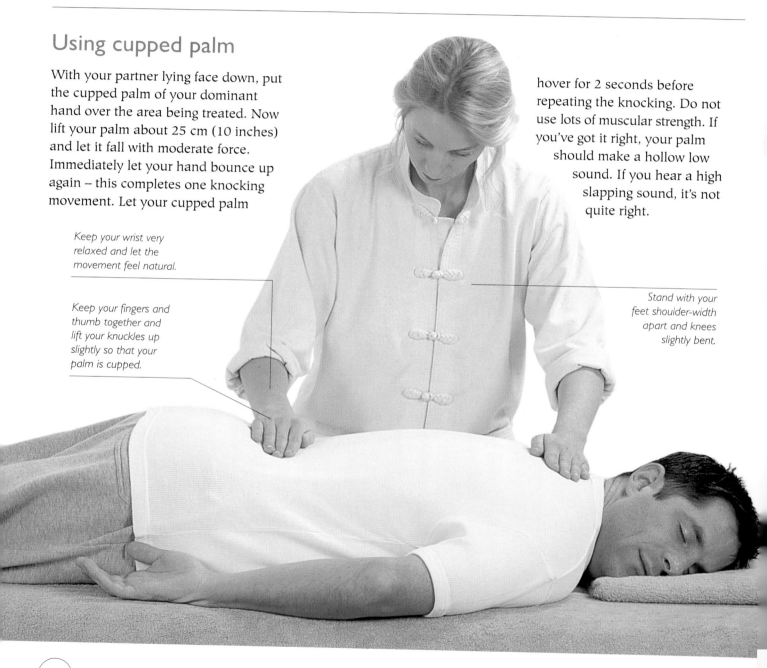

Keep your wrist very relaxed and let the movement feel natural.

Keep your fingers and thumb together and lift your knuckles up slightly so that your palm is cupped.

Stand with your feet shoulder-width apart and knees slightly bent.

Using hollow fist

This can be applied in two ways: with the little-finger edge of your hand and with the middle sections of your fingers. For both, you must curl your thumb and fingers in towards your palm loosely to make a hollow fist. Stand with your feet shoulder-width apart, knees bent, spine straight and shoulders relaxed. Place your empty fist on the area to be treated, then lift it up a few inches and let it fall down. Lift it back up straight away as if it is bouncing off the body.

Knock softly – do not use any force. Work at a moderate speed, keeping relaxed and pausing briefly between each knock.

Method one
Knock with the middle sections of your fingers, as if you were knocking on a door. With this method, you can use both fists alternately and rhythmically on the area being treated.

Keep your wrist flexible and relaxed, and your arm graceful.

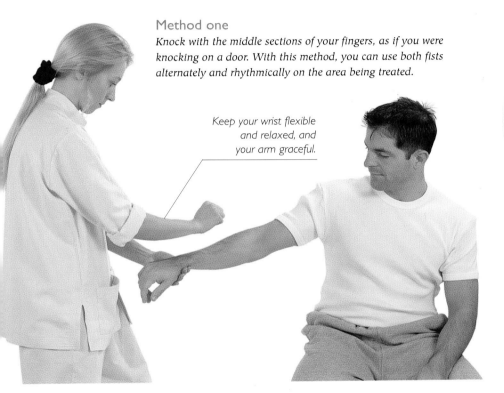

Method two
Knock with the little-finger edge of your palm and an upright hollow fist.

Tips for practice

- Keep your wrist very pliable – do not stiffen up.
- Work slowly, in a relaxed manner.
- Let your palm or fist bounce naturally off the body. Do not be heavy handed.
- In palm knocking, keep your fingers together and palm cupped and listen for the low hollow sound.
- In fist knocking, keep your fist loose. Do not clench it tightly.
- Knock 3–10 times on any one area.

Where on the body? The cupped palm method is used mainly on the back (particularly the lower lumbar vertebrae and sacrum at the end of a treatment); it is also used on the shoulders, thighs and ribs. The little-finger edge of your fist is used mainly on the head and shoulders. The middle sections of your fingers are used on the back, joints, arms and legs.

What are the effects? Relaxes muscles and tendons, clears heat, calms mind, quells fire, clears meridians, promotes Qi and blood circulation, moves blood stasis, regulates functions of stomach and intestines, opens chest, aids breathing, relieves muscle spasm, eases pain.

What can it treat? Headaches, dizziness, difficulty breathing, coughs, nausea, vomiting, lower back ache, shoulder pain and various musculoskeletal ailments.

Che Fa *squeezing tweaking*

掐
挤
法

Che fa is a very straightforward technique used mainly to stimulate points along the major meridians and also along sections of the meridians in lines. It is performed with the ends of the pads of the thumb and index finger, and is applied until the surface of the skin at the point or area being treated becomes red. Practise on points on your own forearm and hand and, when you have the feel of it, work on your partner. For added stimulation, add a quick twisting movement as you release the skin.

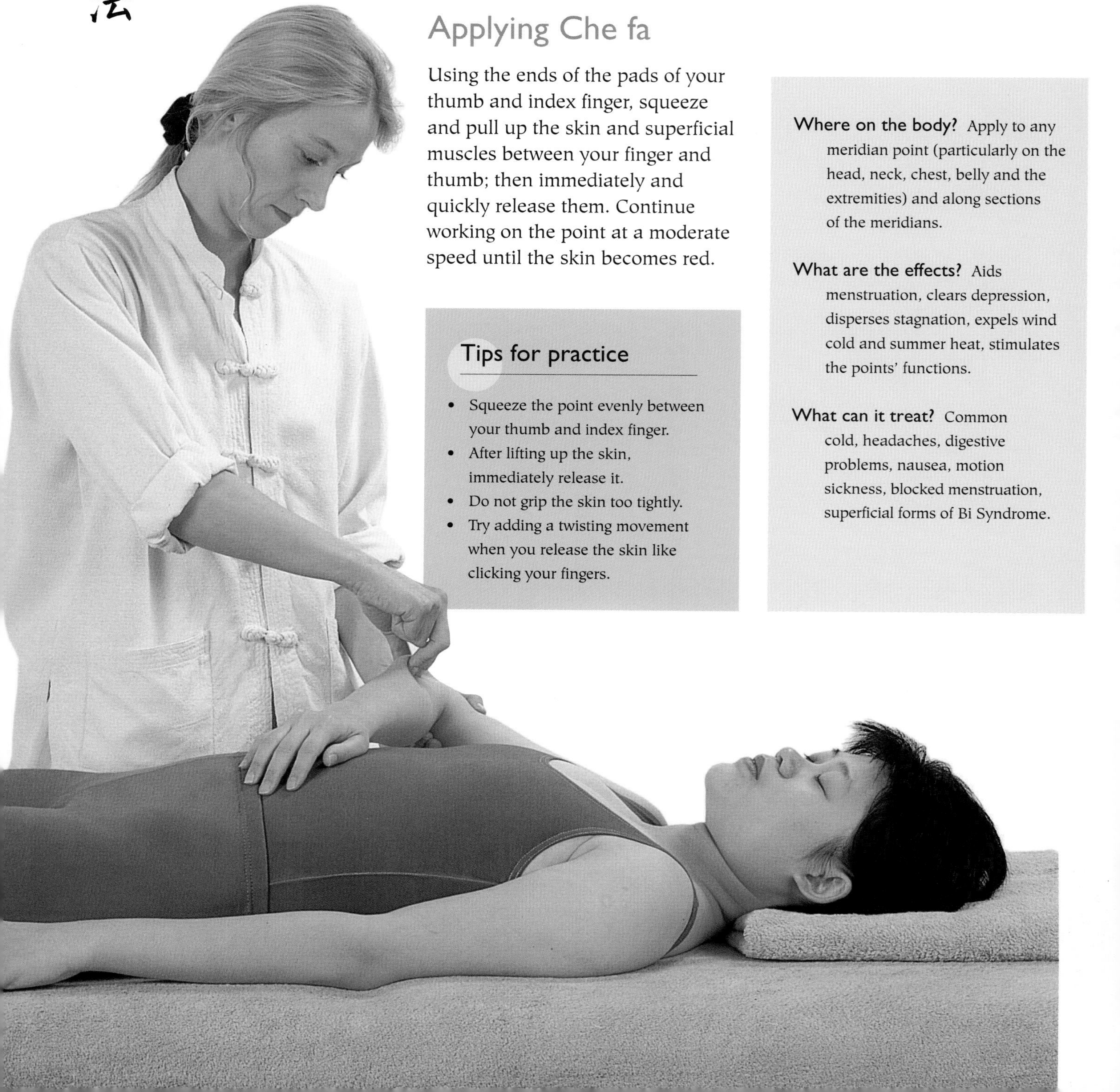

Applying Che fa

Using the ends of the pads of your thumb and index finger, squeeze and pull up the skin and superficial muscles between your finger and thumb; then immediately and quickly release them. Continue working on the point at a moderate speed until the skin becomes red.

Where on the body? Apply to any meridian point (particularly on the head, neck, chest, belly and the extremities) and along sections of the meridians.

What are the effects? Aids menstruation, clears depression, disperses stagnation, expels wind cold and summer heat, stimulates the points' functions.

What can it treat? Common cold, headaches, digestive problems, nausea, motion sickness, blocked menstruation, superficial forms of Bi Syndrome.

Tips for practice

- Squeeze the point evenly between your thumb and index finger.
- After lifting up the skin, immediately release it.
- Do not grip the skin too tightly.
- Try adding a twisting movement when you release the skin like clicking your fingers.

Nian Fa *holding twisting*

Nian fa is used only on the fingers and toes. It is applied with the thumb and index finger or thumb, index, middle and ring fingers, depending on what feels most comfortable to you. Nian fa is quite easy to apply and you can practise on your partner straight away. I generally use it towards the end of treatment if I'm working on a problem connected to any of the joints in the limbs as well as for local problems of the hand or foot. It helps to stimulate the flow of Qi and rounds the treatment off.

Applying Nian fa

Hold your partner's finger between the palm surface of your thumb and index finger (or first three fingers) and twist it quite quickly. Do not work superficially – hold the digit firmly, moving the underlying joints and muscles. You can move the twisting gradually from the root to the tip of the finger, or remain at one particular joint. Work each finger several times. Use the same principles if working on the toes.

Tips for practice

- Keep your fingers pliable and relaxed.
- Imagine you are polishing a coin between your thumb and fingers.
- Be firm and work quickly.
- Work each finger several times.
- Coordinate the twisting evenly between your thumb and finger.

Where on the body? Apply to the fingers and toes.

What are the effects? Stops swelling, eases and opens joints, alleviates pain, relaxes muscles and tendons, promotes Qi and blood circulation.

What can it treat? Sprains, swelling, numbness and pain in fingers and toes. Also used as a supplementary technique for musculoskeletal problems of the limbs and repetitive sprain injury.

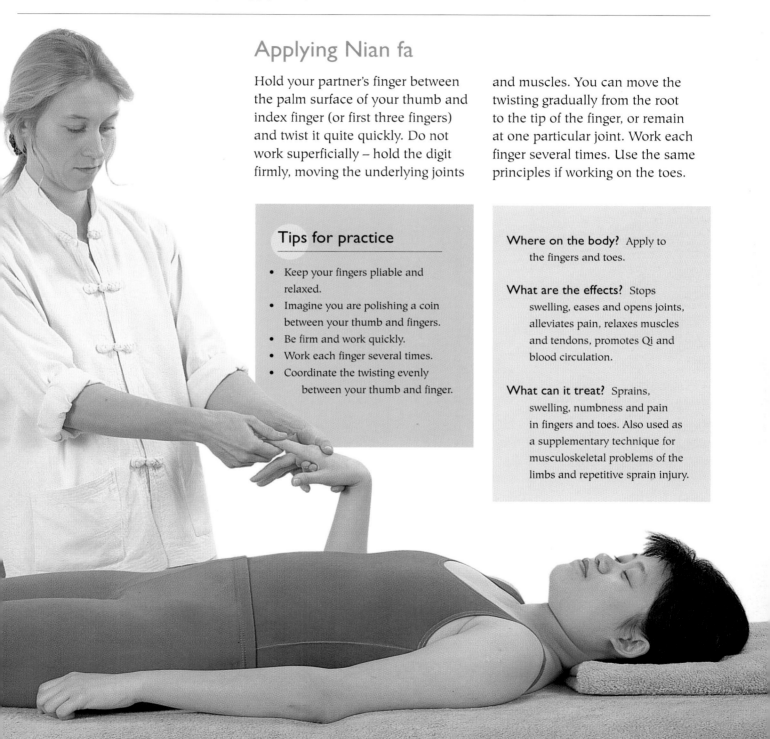

Related Techniques

Professional Tui Na practitioners often incorporate the use of two further therapeutic methods into their overall treatment, as appropriate. These therapies are cupping and moxibustion. For example, I was treating a patient who was suffering with chronic frozen shoulder on both sides. I applied cups to one shoulder to relax the muscles and bring the stagnation to the surface of the skin, while I massaged the other shoulder. After 15 minutes I changed sides.

Moxibustion is of great use to the Tui Na practitioner. It can be used to stimulate and warm individual points or larger areas. I use the technique frequently in practice to move stagnant Qi and blood when treating musculoskeletal problems. In cases of Yang deficiency and internal cold, moxibustion is an essential part of treatment. On the other hand, one should never use moxa on an individual with any signs of heat, such as bright-red tongue, rapid pulse, thirst and fever.

Cupping

Once the cups are in place, they can be moved up and down along the surface of the skin. After cupping, the skin becomes reddish purple; this disappears after a few days.

Moxibustion

Here a moxa stick is held near the skin and moved in circles, lines or pecking movements. Moxibustion is pleasant to experience, feeling like the sun beating down on your body, and most people find it relaxing.

Cupping moves stagnant Qi and blood and expels exterior pathogens, such as wind and damp. It is often applied for asthma, colds and flu, backache and various musculoskeletal ailments.

Cupping involves the application of glass or bamboo cups to the surface of the skin. The cups are applied by taking the oxygen out of the cup with the use of a flame. A piece of cotton wool soaked in surgical spirit is held by long forceps and ignited. The cup is held near the area of skin to be treated, the flame is put inside the cup and then withdrawn, leaving a vacuum. The cup is then immediately placed onto the skin, creating a suction. Cups are normally left in place for 5–15 minutes. The cups are removed by pressing down on the skin near to the rim of the cup, thus allowing air in.

Moxibustion is the burning of moxa – a herb similar to mugwort – as a warming treatment. It is applied for conditions such as Yang deficiency and excess cold and for strengthening Qi and blood.

Moxa is often used in the form of a stick and held close to the surface of the skin. Loose moxa is also formed into cone shapes and applied either directly onto the skin or indirectly on ginger, garlic or salt. The moxa is ignited and smoulders, a bit like incense. A moxa box is sometimes used over larger areas. For this, cones are burnt over a wire mesh inside the box.

The Chinese encourage the regular use of moxa on St 36 to stimulate Qi and keep the immune system strong. It is also very effective for period pain and is applied by moving a moxa stick back and forth above the sacrum.

Applying What You Have Learned

You have now been introduced to twenty Tui Na techniques that are commonly used by practitioners of this branch of traditional Chinese medicine to treat a wide range of ailments.

As you have seen, some of these techniques, such as Gun fa, Yi zhi chan tui fa and Zhen fa, are difficult to master and require a good deal of practice and patience to get them just right. Other techniques, like Mo fa and Rou fa, are quite easy to acquire and you should be able to make use of them almost immediately.

All the Tui Na techniques you have learnt are safe to use at home on your friends and family. However, there are a few important points and contraindications that you should remember.

Points to remember

- Practise the difficult techniques on a daily basis; after a few weeks you will notice a great improvement and after a few months they will start to become second nature.
- Always keep an eye on your posture: keep your spine straight and be as relaxed as possible.
- Develop your strength, stamina and internal force by practising the Qi Gong exercises *(see pages 57–65)*.
- Be patient with yourself.
- Don't get too serious. Have some fun with it – the best learning often comes through play!
- When practising on your partner, think about what you are doing in terms of their Qi and blood and their Yin and Yang. Use your imagination – it is a powerful tool.

Tui Na contraindications

If you feel in any way concerned or worried about giving treatment to someone, it is better not to. Advise them to see a qualified health practitioner.

Avoid applying Tui Na to:

- Anyone who is very hungry or who has just eaten a big meal.
- Anyone who is intoxicated or extremely tired.

Never Apply Tui Na to:

- The affected areas of anyone with a skin disease, such as psoriasis or eczema. The same applies to burns, bruises, boils and other skin injuries.
- Anyone with cancer.
- Anyone with an acute infectious disease.
- The belly or lower back of a pregnant woman. I advise you not to treat pregnant women. Although Tui Na is used during pregnancy, it is best left to a qualified practitioner.
- Anyone with severe mental/emotional problems.
- Anyone with tuberculosis.
- Anyone who is bleeding.
- Anyone who is in a critical condition.
- Anyone who has recently had surgery.

PART THREE

Treating Common Ailments

Having explored the basic theory of traditional Chinese medicine and practised some of the fundamental Tui Na techniques, this part of the book brings the two together. You will now learn how to give simplified Tui Na treatments for some of the most common ailments we encounter.

The following Tui Na treatments for common ailments are simple to follow. Each is divided into its major patterns of disharmony. Check the symptoms to see which pattern your patient fits in to. It is not possible to include every pattern for the ailments discussed; for more detailed information, refer to a specialized practitioner's textbook (*see Further reading, page 139*).

Do not expect the people you treat to fit perfectly with a pattern – everyone is unique. It is far more likely that he or she will express three or four major symptoms of a pattern and a variety of other symptoms not listed. Always check the tongue and feel the pulse for further clarification. Diagnosis in Chinese medicine requires flexibility, intuition and knowledge. It is an art that takes many years of practice, study and observation to master. There is an old Chinese saying, 'Intuition without knowledge is dangerous, knowledge without intuition is useless'.

One of the most important factors to work out is whether the person you are treating has a pattern of excess or one of deficiency. Look back at the section on the eight guiding principles (*see pages 26–9*) to remind yourself of this.

Once you have diagnosed your patient, you can follow the relevant treatment. The small photographs included in these step-by-step treatments serve to remind you of each technique as it appears. You may need to refer back to part two until you are familiar with all the techniques. Each treatment also includes the stimulation of important points. The quick-reference diagrams will remind you where these are, but again, you may need to check back to part one (*see pages 48–53*) for exact locations.

When giving treatments, always remember to keep the treatment principle (such as, 'tonify the spleen and resolve damp') in mind. Your intention during treatment can have a powerful effect. Also, keep your inner attention on the part of your hand that you are using to apply a technique and imagine Qi moving through you and into the body of the person you are treating.

Common Colds

In Chinese medicine there are various types of common cold. Many of the familiar symptoms, such as sneezing, blocked nose, sore throat and headaches, are caused by exterior wind from the environment invading the lungs via the skin and nose, and obstructing the lungs' function of descending and dispersing Qi.

The Chinese say that 'wind is the spearhead of disease'. It is thought of as both actual wind (the weather) and any sudden change in temperature. This could mean, for example, going from standing outside on a cold day to entering a central-heated house or, in the summer, coming from a hot journey to work into an air-conditioned office. Wind is Yang by nature and generally combines with and drives other exterior environmental factors with it into the body, such as cold, heat and damp.

Below are three of the most frequently encountered types of common cold, with an outline of the signs and symptoms to look for and a treatment principle for each. Overleaf are step-by-step treatments for each type of cold.

You will find the massage media dong qing gao and ginger and spring onion tincture useful in treating wind cold, wind heat and damp invading the lungs. (*Recipes are given for each on page 56.*)

PATTERN TO BE TREATED: Wind cold invading the lungs

Causes	Signs and symptoms	Treatment principle	Course of treatment
Cold in the environment combines with wind and invades the body, obstructing the lungs' function of descending and dispersing Qi.	Aversion to cold, fever, itchy throat, blocked or runny nose, clear watery mucus, sneezing, achy body, cough, headache.	Release the exterior, expel wind, scatter cold and stimulate the descending and dispersing function of the lungs.	1 treatment per day for 3 days. 1 day's break, then 1 treatment per day for a further 3 days.

	Tongue	*Pulse*	
	Thin white coating	Superficial, floating and tight	

PATTERN TO BE TREATED: Wind heat invading the lungs

Causes	Signs and symptoms	Treatment principle	Course of treatment
Exterior heat from the environment combines with wind and invades the body. In practice it is very common to see an invasion of wind cold turning into wind heat, as cold quickly turns to heat once it has entered the body. Central heating can be the cause of this.	Sore throat, slight sweating, cough, aversion to cold or wind, headache, blocked or runny nose, yellow mucus, achy body, thirst, swollen tonsils.	Release the exterior, expel wind, clear heat, stimulate the descending and dispersing function of the lungs.	1 treatment per day for 3 days. 1 day's break, then 1 treatment per day for a further 3 days.

	Tongue	*Pulse*	
	Body of the tongue red towards the tip, and thin white or yellow coating	Rapid and superficial or floating	

PATTERN TO BE TREATED: Wind cold and damp invading the lungs

Causes

Wind combines with cold and damp and invades the body, obstructing the lungs' function of controlling the water passages. This can result in symptoms of swelling in addition to the respiratory symptoms.

Signs and symptoms

Fever, swelling of the face and eyes which can spread to the rest of the body, muzzy head, aversion to cold and/or wind, coughing, an oppressive feeling in the epigastrium (upper belly).

Tongue

White greasy coating

Pulse

Superficial floating and slippery

Treatment principle

Release the exterior, scatter cold, resolve damp, stimulate the descending and dispersing function of the lungs and open the water passages.

Course of treatment

1 treatment per day for 3 days. 1 day's break, then 1 treatment per day for a further 3 days.

General advice

Getting enough sleep and rest is important. It is common in practice to see patients with colds continuing to push themselves, ignoring the signs of disharmony they are experiencing or trying to repress them. This can lead to a weakening of the individual's defensive Qi and further invasions are likely. The exterior environmental factors of wind, cold, heat and damp must be released, scattered, resolved or cleared, or they can move deeper into the body, creating more serious patterns of disharmony and a further depletion of the individual's energetic system.

Diet

While you have cold symptoms, it is best to avoid dairy products as they form damp. Too much dairy produce is likely to make the cold linger on, especially the mucus. Oranges and orange juice, much to people's surprise, are also to be avoided; they are by nature hot and damp and have a tendency to form phlegm in the body. It is better to take a good vitamin C supplement than to drink vast quantities of orange juice. Generally, while cold symptoms are present, eat a light diet – soups are good – and don't overfill yourself.

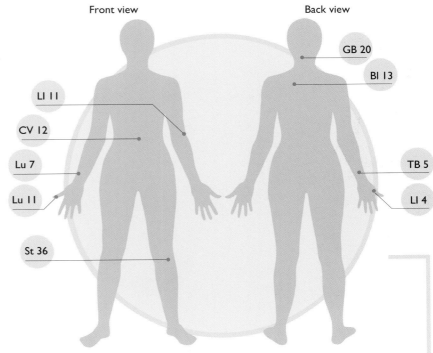

Front view — Back view

LI 11, CV 12, Lu 7, Lu 11, St 36, GB 20, Bl 13, TB 5, LI 4

Quick point-finder for common colds

You will find the points highlighted here used in the treatment of colds shown overleaf. These diagrams are a quick reminder *(for exact point location see pages 48–53)*.

Simple treatments for the common cold

These step-by-step treatments cover the colds described on the previous two pages. All these techniques are covered in detail in part two (see page references) and all the points appear in part one. However, as you become more familiar with the techniques, the small pictures here should be enough to guide you. Each technique is photographed the first time it appears. As you work, try to concentrate on the relevant treatment principle.

Treating wind cold invading the lungs

1 Na fa p 74

With your partner seated, use Na fa (grasping) on the back of the neck, with ginger and spring onion tincture (see page 56), from the base of the skull down. Repeat for several minutes until the neck is warm.

2 Yi zhi chan tui fa p 68

Use Yi zhi chan tui fa (one finger meditation) on GB 20 on both sides of the neck for about 3 minutes.

3 Rou fa p 70

Use Rou fa (kneading) with your thumb on Bl 13 on both sides for 3 minutes. Move anticlockwise for a reducing, clearing effect. If you prefer, you can use Yi zhi chan tui fa on this point instead.

4 Tui fa p 80

With your partner lying on their back, stand behind the head and use Tui fa (pushing) with your thumb quite briskly, from Yingtang extra point to the anterior hairline, about 60 times.

5 Ma fa p 81

Use Ma fa (wiping) from the centre of the forehead outwards to the temples and from the eyebrows up to the anterior hairline, briskly, about 60 times.

6 Che fa p 92

Use Che fa (nipping) between the tip of your thumb and index finger on Lu 7 about 30 times on each arm.

7 Yi zhi chan tui fa p 68

Stimulate LI 4 with one finger meditation for 3 minutes on each hand. Na fa can also be used on this point if you prefer.

8 Ca fa ◁ p 76

Ask your partner to lie on their front and use Ca fa (scrubbing) on the bladder meridian both sides of the spine. Use some dong qing gao (see page 56), working from the sacrum to the shoulders until the back is hot.

Treating wind heat invading the lungs

1   Na fa   p 74

With your partner seated, use grasping technique repeatedly on the back of their neck, from the base of the skull down, for several minutes until the neck becomes warm.

4   Yi zhi chan tui fa   p 68

Use one finger meditation on TB 5 and LI 4 for 3 minutes on each side, moving in the direction of your partner's fingertips.

2   Mo fa   p 72

Use Mo fa (round rubbing) to stroke and caress the head. Start slowly and gradually increase speed until it is quite fast and the head feels warm. Work from left to right.

3   Che fa   p 92

Ask your partner to lie on their back. Nip Lu 11 on both sides with your thumb nail for 1 minute.

5   Na fa   p 74

Use Na fa on LI 11 for 3 minutes on each elbow. Then, using the tips of your index fingers, grasp each eyebrow, working outwards 6 times on each one.

Treating wind cold and damp invading the lungs

1   Mo fa   p 72

With your partner seated, use round rubbing to stroke and caress the head. Keep working until it begins to feel warm.

4   Pia fa   p 90

Repeat this, using Pia fa (knocking) with the fingertips down the bladder meridian.

7   An rou fa   p 89

Ask your partner to lie on their back and use An rou fa (revolving) in an anticlockwise direction with your forearm over the navel for several minutes or until the belly feels warm.

2   Na fa   p 74

Use grasping technique (with ginger and spring onion tincture) on the back of the neck, working from the base of the skull down for several minutes until warm.

5   Che fa   p 92

Nip Lu 7 between the tip of your thumb and index finger about 30 times on both sides.

8   Yi zhi chan tui fa   p 68

Use one finger meditation on St 36 on both sides for 3 minutes, directing the movement towards your partner's head.

9   Zhen fa   p 84

Use vibrating technique with your middle finger on CV 12 for 3 minutes.

3   Zhen fa   p 84

Use Zhen fa (vibrating) with the middle finger on the back of the neck. Work down the bladder meridian either side of the neck 3–4 times on both sides.

6   Na fa   p 74

Use grasping technique on LI 4 for 3 minutes on each side.

10   Ji fa △   p 82

Use Ji fa (chopping) with joined palms up and down both legs several times.

Headaches

Tui Na is very effective in treating headaches. It generally gives great on-the-spot relief and, in cases of long-term headaches and migraines, regular treatments over time can create lasting results.

There are many patterns of disharmony associated with headaches and many factors which can lead to these patterns. A person's basic constitution and their emotions are both common causes. Excessive worrying, fear and anger often have a part to play. And working too hard can cause headaches by depleting Qi.

Diet is also an important factor: too little to eat, and Qi and blood can become deficient; too much food can interfere with the stomach and spleen, causing forehead headaches. Excess hot energy foods, such as spices and alcohol, can create heat and fire, leading to headaches.

Accidents and old traumatic injuries cause blood stasis – often a cause of chronic (long-term) headaches.

External environmental factors such as wind, cold, heat and damp can invade the body and cause headaches. Wind, for example, makes the muscles of the neck stiff, obstructing the flow of Qi and blood, leading to headaches. Damp and phlegm can also create obstruction and prevent the clear Yang from rising to the head.

The list of causes is long, and the complexity of our bodies means that these causes often come in combination. It is not possible to look at every single pattern here, so I have chosen three of the most common. Their symptoms and treatment principles are below, with simple step-by-step treatments overleaf.

PATTERN TO BE TREATED: Liver Yang rising

Causes	Signs and symptoms		Treatment principle	Course of treatment
The most likely cause of this type of headache is emotion, in particular any feelings with their roots in anger, such as frustration, guilt and resentment. Expressed or repressed, these can, over time, cause the liver Yang to rebel and rise excessively.	Throbbing, intense headache, usually on the gall bladder meridian at the sides of the head, the temple area or behind the eyes. Often joined by nausea and/or vomiting, sometimes visual disturbance. Other symptoms may be dizziness, tinnitus, deafness, insomnia, feeling tense or irritable.		Subdue liver Yang, nourish Yin.	1 treatment per day for 10 days.
	Tongue	*Pulse*		
	Red, particularly at the sides	Wiry, forceful		

PATTERN TO BE TREATED: Qi deficiency

Causes	Signs and symptoms		Treatment principle	Course of treatment
The Qi of the spleen, stomach, lungs or heart becomes deficient, so there is not enough Qi to ascend to the head.	Headache usually on forehead, although can affect whole head. Dull ache made worse by overwork, better for resting. Often worse in the morning. Other symptoms may be lack of appetite, tiredness, weakness, loose stools, breathlessness.		Tonify and raise Qi.	1 treatment per day for 10 days.
	Tongue	*Pulse*		
	Pale with a thin coating	Weak, feeble		

General advice

For liver Yang rising headaches (this includes migraine), try the exercise below. In deficiency-type headaches, getting enough rest is important – try a short rest in the afternoon. For damp or phlegm headaches, exercise is to be encouraged. Qi Gong is of great help in all cases.

Diet

For damp or phlegm headaches, eliminate excess dairy products and sweet foods. In liver Yang rising headaches, coffee and sour foods should be cut down or eliminated.

Migraine exercise

If done before the headache has come on, this can stop it developing fully. Sit in a quiet place on an upright chair. Take off your shoes and socks and put your feet flat on the floor, a little forward of your knees. Keep your spine straight and place the backs of your hands on your thighs, fingers relaxed. Imagine a thermometer in each hand, and your palms becoming red hot. Try to make the gauge reach maximum. Think of heat moving down your arms from your head to your palms. Do this for about 5 minutes, then stimulate LI 4 then Liv 3 using Na fa (grasping) for several minutes on both sides. The sensation should be a strong aching. Then drink a glass of water.

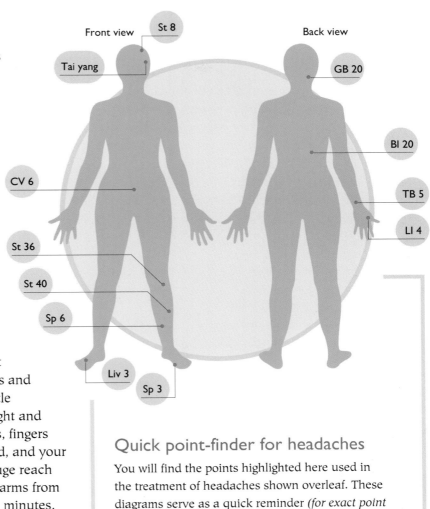

Front view · Back view

St 8 · Tai yang · GB 20 · Bl 20 · CV 6 · TB 5 · LI 4 · St 36 · St 40 · Sp 6 · Liv 3 · Sp 3

Quick point-finder for headaches

You will find the points highlighted here used in the treatment of headaches shown overleaf. These diagrams serve as a quick reminder (for exact point location see pages 48–53).

PATTERN TO BE TREATED: Damp or phlegm obstructing the stomach and spleen

Causes

Common in countries with a damp climate and in individuals with a diet high in damp energy foods, such as dairy products. Damp and phlegm create obstruction and stagnation in the middle burner which spreads upwards to the head.

Signs and symptoms

A dull headache and muzzy feeling in the head. Head feels heavy. Difficulty concentrating and thinking. Often worse in the morning. Whole head or forehead affected. Other symptoms may be a feeling of oppression in the chest and epigastrium, nausea, lack of appetite, dizziness, catarrh.

Tongue

Thick, sticky, greasy coating

Pulse

Slippery

Treatment principle

Resolve damp and phlegm, tonify stomach and spleen.

Course of treatment

1 treatment per day for 10 days.

Simple treatments for headaches

These step-by-step treatments cover the headaches on the previous two pages. All these techniques are covered in detail in part two (see page references) and all the points appear in part one. However, as you become more familiar with the techniques, the small pictures here should be enough to guide you. Each technique is photographed the first time it appears. As you work, try to concentrate on the relevant treatment principle.

Treating liver Yang rising

1 Yi zhi chan tui fa p 68

Use Yi zhi chan tui fa (one-finger meditation) on Liv 3 for 3 minutes on both sides. Direct the movement towards your partner's toes.

2 Mo fa p 72

With your partner seated, use Mo fa to stroke and caress the head, working from left to right, slow to fast until the head feels very warm.

3 Pia fa and Na fa pp 74/90

Standing behind your partner, use Pia fa, with a hollow fist on the crown of her head. At the same time use Na fa (grasping) on top of the shoulder with your other hand. Do this for 2 minutes, then swap hands so the hand that was striking is now grasping the shoulder that hasn't been worked on.

4 Na fa ▽ p 74

Use grasping technique with your five fingers on your partner's head, supporting her forehead with your other hand. Spread your fingers as far as possible to grasp the five meridians of the head. Work from the forehead backwards and grasp down the neck and nape. Do this 5 times.

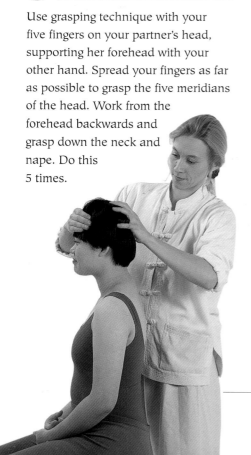

5 Zhen fa p 84

Use Zhen fa (vibrating) on GB 20 for 3 minutes on both sides. If you prefer, Yi zhi chan tui fa could be used to stimulate this point.

6 Rou fa p 70

Use Rou fa (kneading) with your thumb on the back of your partner's neck. Work from the base of the skull down to the nape on both sides of the spine. Do this 4 times. Then, use Rou fa on Tai yang extra point for 3 minutes on both sides.

7 Cuo fa p 75

Use Cuo fa (rub rolling) down the arms – twice on each arm. Then rub roll the ribs (pictured here). Work from the armpits to the lower ribs 3 times.

8 Yi zhi chan tui fa p 68

Use one finger meditation on TB 5 for 3 minutes on both sides, directing the movement towards your partner's fingers.

Treating Qi deficiency

1 Mo fa p 72

With your partner on their back, use clockwise round rubbing with joined palms on the abdomen for 3 minutes.

2 Zhen fa p 84

Use vibrating technique with one finger on CV 6 for 3 minutes.

3 Yi zhi chan tui fa p 68

Use one finger meditation on St 36 and Sp 6 for 3 minutes on both sides. Think about projecting Qi into the points.

4 Tui fa p 80

Ask your partner to lie on their front and use Tui fa (pushing) with the whole of both palms down the back, along the bladder meridian either side of the spine until the back feels hot. You can use some dong qing gao *(see page 56)* on the skin for this.

5 Yi zhi chan tui fa p 68

Use one finger meditation on Bl 20 for 3 minutes on both sides.

6 Pia fa p 90

With your partner seated, strike with a hollow fist on their crown for 2 minutes.

7 Na fa p 74

Use grasping technique on both shoulders for several minutes.

8 Ma fa p 81

Use Ma fa (wiping) with your thumbs on your partner's forehead, from the eyebrows to hairline several times.

Treating damp or phlegm obstructing the stomach and spleen

1 Ji fa p 82

With your partner lying on their back, use Ji fa (dotting) all over the chest for about 3 minutes.

2 Zhen fa p 84

Use vibrating technique with your middle finger and/or palm all over the chest for 3 minutes.

3 An fa p 78

Use An fa (pressing) with the heel of your palm on the chest, working down the chest in lines.

4 An rou fa p 89

Use An rou fa (revolving) with your forearm on the middle and lower abdomen. Work briskly in an anticlockwise direction.

5 Yi zhi chan tui fa p 68

Use one finger meditation on St 40 and Sp 3 for 3 minutes on both sides. Make the technique very strong and vigorous.

6 Mo fa p 72

With your partner seated, use Mo fa to stroke and caress the head until the whole head feels warm.

7 Na fa p 74

Use grasping technique on the back of the neck for several minutes.

8 Ji fa p 82

Chop with joined palms over the upper back and shoulders for 3 minutes.

9 Zhen fa p 84

Use vibrating technique on St 8 for 3 minutes on both sides.

10 Che fa p 92

Use Che fa (nipping) on LI 4 on both sides for 3 minutes.

Insomnia

Insomnia is far more common than we may think and can have a severely debilitating effect on those who suffer from it. As with most ailments in Chinese medicine, there are many patterns of disharmony that can lead to insomnia.

Lifestyle factors are the number one cause. For example, the combination of extreme stress, lack of rest, working long hours and having an irregular diet – all of which are quite common in a fast-pace city life – can deplete the kidney Yin. Over a period of time, the Yin of the kidney becomes so deficient that it can no longer nourish the Yin of the heart. The heart has the function of housing the mind which, in good health, is rooted in the heart blood and Yin. If it loses these roots, the mind suffers and sleep is easily affected.

Emotions such as worry, anxiety, anger and frustration can create fire within the body, particularly in the heart and liver. Fire has a natural tendency to rise up towards the head and can agitate the mind, causing insomnia.

In Chinese medicine, it is said that the ethereal soul (Hun) resides in the liver Yin and blood. If blood becomes deficient, the ethereal soul loses its home and, at night, begins to float and wander, causing a very restless sleep and vivid, exhausting dreams. Cases like this are often seen in individuals who have experienced a large loss of blood, such as during childbirth. Over the next few pages you will find signs and symptoms, treatment principles and simple Tui Na treatments for three common types of insomnia.

PATTERN TO BE TREATED: Spleen and heart blood deficiency

Causes	Signs and symptoms		Treatment principle	Course of treatment
This is one of the most common patterns related to insomnia. Blood has become deficient, possibly due to overwork, poor diet or loss of blood.	Difficulty getting off to sleep, but once asleep will stay asleep. Other symptoms may be palpitations, dizziness, tiredness, anxiety, lack of appetite, pale complexion, poor memory, blurred vision.		Tonify the spleen, nourish blood, nourish the heart and calm the mind.	1 treatment per day for 10 days.

Tongue	*Pulse*
Pale	Weak

PATTERN TO BE TREATED: Heart and kidney Yin deficiency

Causes	Signs and symptoms		Treatment principle	Course of treatment
The Yin of the kidneys has become deficient and fails to nourish the Yin of the heart, so the mind is robbed of its residence.	Difficulty falling asleep and waking several times in the night. Other symptoms may be: night sweating, dry throat, backache around waist level or lumbar area, tinnitus, restlessness, feeling of heat in chest, palms and soles of feet.		Nourish Yin, tonify the heart and kidneys, clear empty heat and calm the mind.	1 treatment per day for 10 days; continue with another course if needed.

Tongue	*Pulse*
Red, particularly at the tip, dry with little or no coating	Thready and rapid

General advice

The Qi Gong exercise 'Standing for health' *(see page 59)* is very effective for insomnia. Practise for 5 minutes in the morning and again before going to bed. It is also important to empty the mind before sleeping. Try the relaxation and breathing exercises below. There are lots of tapes available to aid relaxation. Hypnotherapy is also very effective and meditation is invaluable.

Diet

Eating rich, heavy foods late at night is to be avoided, as are coffee and tea. If there is phlegm present, cut down dairy, fatty and sugary foods. If heat is present, avoid spices, curries and alcohol.

Relaxation exercise

Starting from the toes and working up to the head, talk your body into relaxation. For example, start by saying, 'The toes of my right foot relax, melt, let go. The top of my foot release, let go, relax. My whole foot melts and is totally relaxed.' Continue in this way up your body.

Breathing exercise

Try regulating your breathing. Keeping your attention on your lower belly, breathe in through your nose for 4 counts, hold for 2 counts and breathe out through your mouth for 8 counts. Work like this for about 5 minutes.

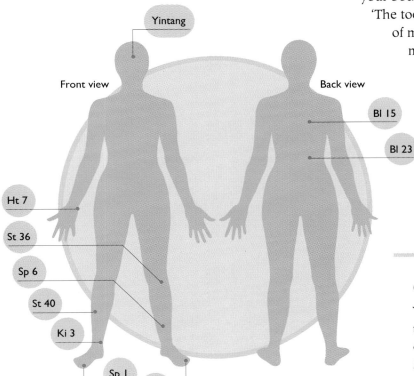

Yintang

Front view

Back view

Bl 15

Bl 23

Ht 7

St 36

Sp 6

St 40

Ki 3

Sp 1

St 45

Quick point-finder for insomnia

You will find the points highlighted here used in the treatment of insomnia shown overleaf. These diagrams are a quick reminder *(for exact point location see pages 48–53)*.

PATTERN TO BE TREATED: Phlegm-heat harassing the mind				
Causes	**Signs and symptoms**		**Treatment principle**	**Course of treatment**
Stomach Qi rebels upwards, carrying with it phlegm and heat which interfere with the heart and mind, leading to insomnia.	Restless sleep, constantly tossing and turning with difficult dreams. Other symptoms may be: dizziness, heavy feeling in body, full feeling in chest and/or epigastrium, lack of appetite, nausea, mental unease, sticky taste in the mouth.		Clear heat, resolve phlegm, calm the mind.	1 treatment per day for 2 weeks and a further course if needed.
	Tongue Red with sticky or greasy thick yellow coating	*Pulse* Rapid and slippery		

Simple treatments for insomnia

These step-by-step treatments cover the patterns of insomnia described on the previous two pages. All these techniques are covered in detail in part two (*see page references*) and all the points appear in part one. However, as you become more familiar with the techniques, the small pictures here should be enough to guide you. Each technique is shown the first time it appears. As you work, try to concentrate on the treatment principle.

Treating spleen and heart blood deficiency

1 Tui fa   p 80

With your partner lying on their front, use Tui fa (pushing) with the palms of both your hands down the bladder meridian on the back, either side of the spine. Do this repeatedly until the back feels very warm.

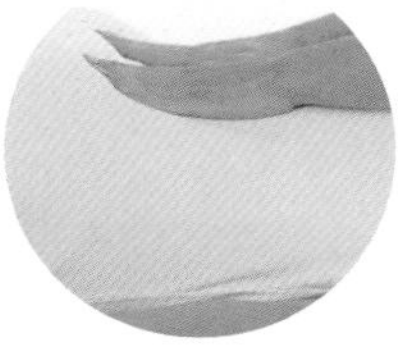

2 Na fa   p 74

Use Na fa (grasping) down the bladder meridian either side of the spine. Do this about 6 times on each side.

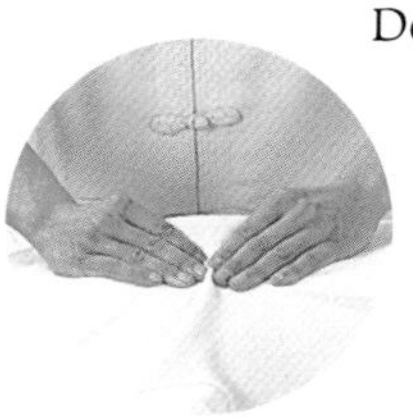

3 An rou fa   p 89

Use An rou fa (revolving) with your forearm on the back at the level of the waist in a clockwise direction for about 3 minutes or until the area becomes warm.

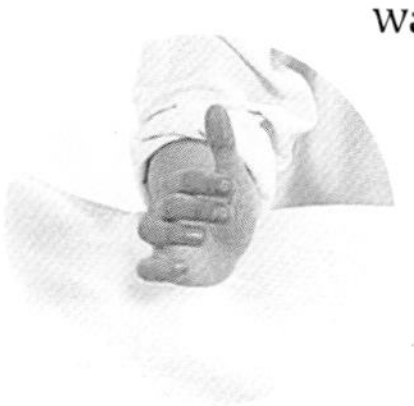

4 Che fa   p 92

Ask your partner to turn onto their back. Use Che fa (tweaking) on the eyebrows, working from the inner to the outer corner, one eyebrow at a time. Do this 9 times on each eyebrow.

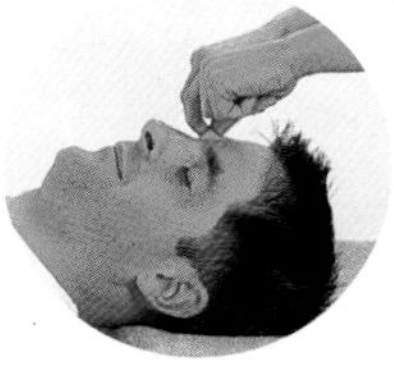

5 Zhen fa   p 84

Apply Zhen fa (vibrating) on Yintang extra point for 3 minutes using your middle finger.

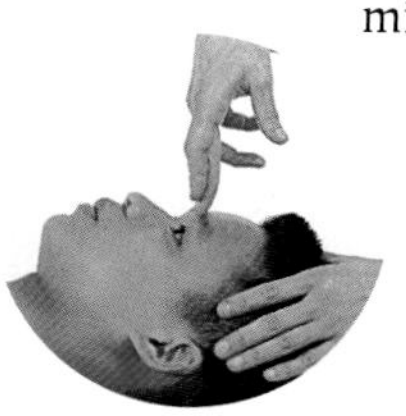

6 Ca fa ▽   p 76

Use Ca fa (scrubbing) with the heels of your palms on the temples and sides of the head until warm.

7 Zhen fa   p 84

Apply vibrating technique on Ht 7 for 3 minutes using your middle finger on both sides.

8 An fa   p 78

Use An fa (pressing) with your thumb on St 36 (*pictured here*) for 3 minutes. Then use An fa on Sp 6 for 3 minutes. Repeat on the other leg. (If you prefer, use Yi zhi chan tui fa to stimulate these points.)

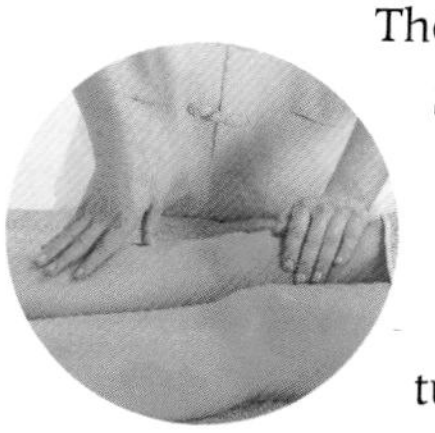

Treating heart and kidney Yin deficiency

1 **Mo fa** p 72

With your partner seated, use Mo fa to stroke and caress the head. Work from left to right, front to back, slow to fast, until the whole head feels hot.

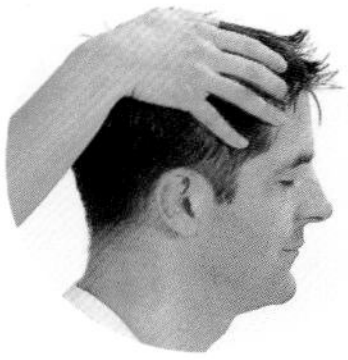

2 **Na fa** p 74

Use grasping technique on the back of the neck for several minutes until it feels warm.

3 **Zhen fa** p 84

Ask your partner to lie down on their front and use vibrating technique (or, alternatively, use An fa) on Bl 23 and Bl 15 for 3 minutes on both sides.

4 **Ca fa** ▷ p 76

Use Ca fa (scrubbing) horizontally across the back at waist level until hot. Then use Ca fa to scratch the back down the bladder meridian *(pictured here)* both sides of the spine until hot.

5 **Zhen fa** p 84

Ask your partner to turn onto their back. Apply vibrating technique on Ht 7 and Ki 3 for 3 minutes on both sides, using your middle finger. Then use vibrating technique with the palm of your hand on the lower abdomen.

Treating phlegm-heat harassing the mind

1 **Ji fa** p 82

With your partner lying down on their front, use Ji fa (chopping) with joined palms all over the back and shoulders. Do this several times.

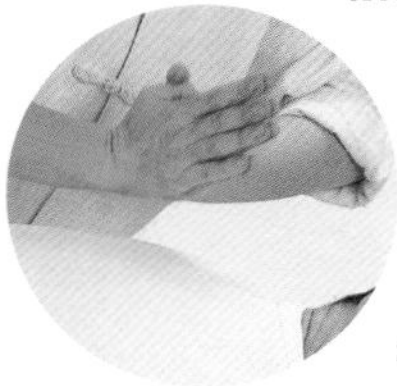

2 **Pia fa** p 90

Apply Pia fa (knocking), using an empty, cupped palm all over the back. Work like this for 2–3 minutes.

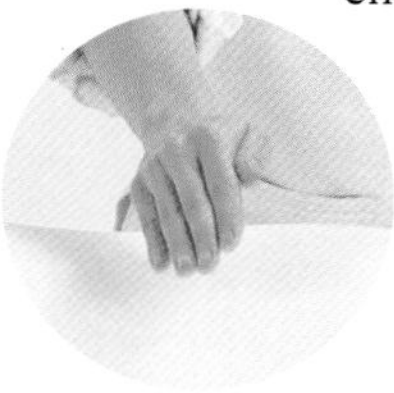

3 **Ji fa** p 82

Apply chopping technique with separate palms all over the backs of the legs. Work up and down each leg several times.

4 **Tui fa** p 80

Ask your partner to turn onto their back. Use pushing technique with both palms down the abdomen, working from the ribs towards the pubic bone. Work quite briskly and do this many times until the belly feels warm.

5 **Mo fa** p 72

Use round rubbing on the abdomen with the palm of your hand. Work in an anticlockwise circle for about 3 minutes.

6 **Gun fa** p 66

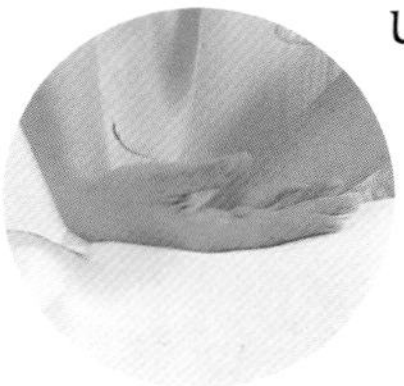

Use Gun fa (rolling) on the abdomen for several minutes. Work briskly but not too heavily.

7 **Yi zhi chan tui fa** p 68

Use one finger meditation on St 40 for 3 minutes on both sides. Work strongly and quickly, directing the movement up the body.

8 **Zhen fa** p 84

Use vibrating technique with your middle finger on Sp 6 for 3 minutes on both sides.

9 **Che fa** p 92

Nip St 45 and Sp 1 for 3 minutes on both sides.

Painful Periods

Painful periods are so commonplace that they are, unfortunately, seen as a normal part of many women's lives. It is rare to find a woman who has never experienced period pain of any kind. Pain can occur just before, during or after the period and is usually felt in the lower belly, lower back and sacrum, or around the waist level. The type of pain varies from woman to woman and can range from a mild, dragging ache to an unbearably intense, stabbing pain. The pain can also be accompanied by other symptoms, such as sweating, nausea and vomiting. Painful periods can have a very disabling effect, leaving a woman unable to go about normal day to day business.

In terms of Chinese medicine, there are several patterns of disharmony that can lead to period pain. The most common is stagnation of liver Qi and blood. The liver controls the smooth flow of Qi, and Qi is the commander of blood, in that its force moves blood through the body. So, if Qi stagnates, blood also stagnates and congeals.

One of the most relevant factors causing painful periods is emotional strain. A build-up of frustration, anger, resentment and guilt can cause liver Qi to stagnate. This, in turn, leads to stagnation of blood in the uterus. An accumulation of cold and damp can also cause blood to stagnate in the uterus. Other causative factors may be having children very close together without adequate time to recuperate, miscarriage, excessive physical work or exercise, lack of exercise, too much or too little sexual activity, and chronic illness.

With regular treatments, Tui Na can produce excellent, lasting results for women who suffer with painful periods. It can also bring great on-the-spot relief. Opposite are three of the most common patterns of disharmony. For each, I have given the signs and symptoms to look for and prescribed a simple step-by-step treatment overleaf.

General advice

In the case of stagnation of Qi and blood, exercise is important. Walking, swimming, yoga and Qi Gong all help to invigorate the flow of Qi and blood, and can reduce pain. If emotional issues are the root of the pains, it may be useful for your patient to see a counsellor or to find a class where she can express her feelings creatively: dance, drumming and voice work are all excellent channels for emotions.

In the case of cold and damp, it is important to take care during and just after a period not to be excessively exposed to these factors. For example, do not walk with

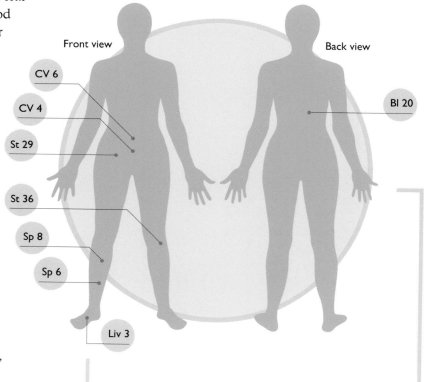

Front view

Back view

CV 6

CV 4

St 29

St 36

Sp 8

Sp 6

Bl 20

Liv 3

Quick point-finder for painful periods

You will find the points highlighted here used in the treatment of period pain shown overleaf. These diagrams are a quick reminder (for exact point location see pages 48–53).

bare feet on cold surfaces or damp grass, as damp tends to invade through the meridians in the legs and settles in the lower burner, where the uterus lives.

Breathing exercise

Learning to breathe properly from your belly will help Qi and blood circulation. Try this simple exercise. Put one hand on your belly and the other on your sacrum (at the same level on your back). Imagine you are breathing into the space between your hands, or into your lower back, and your belly will naturally expand. Breathe in for 4 counts, hold for 4 counts and breathe out for 4. As you breathe out, deliberately pull your lower belly in gently and gradually towards your spine.

PATTERN TO BE TREATED: Stagnation of Qi and blood

Causes	Signs and symptoms	Treatment principle	Course of treatment
Liver Qi stagnates which leads to stagnation of blood in the uterus, causing pain.	Pain and distension or bloating in lower belly before or during period. Tender, distended breasts. Hesitant start to period. Dark blood with clots, pain alleviated by passing of clots, premenstrual tension and irritability, headaches.	Promote the smooth flow of Qi and blood, eliminate stasis, stop pain.	1 treatment per day or every other day for 3 days, a break of 3 days then repeat.

	Tongue	*Pulse*		
	Purple	Wiry, taut, stringy		

PATTERN TO BE TREATED: Stagnation of cold and damp

Causes	Signs and symptoms	Treatment principle	Course of treatment
Exterior cold and damp invade the uterus causing blood to stagnate. Women are susceptible to this during and just after a period, when blood and the uterus are at their lowest ebb.	Pain and a cold feeling in the lower belly before or during the period, pain in the lower back and waist. Pain may be alleviated by warmth. Scanty blood flow, dark blood and dark clots, dislike of cold, loose stools.	Expel cold, resolve damp, warm the uterus, stop pain.	1 treatment per day or every other day for 3 days; a break of 3 days then repeat.

	Tongue	*Pulse*		
	Pale with white, greasy coating	Deep, tight		

PATTERN TO BE TREATED: Qi and blood deficiency

Causes	Signs and symptoms	Treatment principle	Course of treatment
Qi and blood become weak through poor diet, overexertion or chronic illness. There is no force to move blood which leads to a deficient type of stagnation and pain.	Lingering dull pain in the lower belly during or after the period, dragging feeling in the lower belly. Pain is relieved with pressure. Pale, watery blood, pale complexion, tiredness, listlessness, loose stools.	Tonify Qi and nourish blood.	1 treatment per day or every other day for 3 days. A break of 3 days, then repeat.

	Tongue	*Pulse*		
	Pale with a thin white coating	Weak, deep, thready		

Simple treatments for painful periods

These treatments cover the patterns of period pain described on the previous two pages. All the techniques are covered in detail in part two *(see page references)* and all the points appear in part one. However, as you work, try to concentrate on the treatment principle.

become more familiar with the techniques, the small pictures here should be enough to guide you. Each technique is shown the first time it appears. As you work, try to concentrate on the treatment principle.

Treating stagnation of Qi and blood

1 Mo fa   p 72

With your partner lying down on her back, use Mo fa (round rubbing) on her abdomen with your palm, first clockwise then anticlockwise for 5–10 minutes.

2 Yi zhi chan tui fa   p 68

Use Yi zhi chan tui fa (one finger meditation) on CV 6 for 3 minutes. The movement should be in the direction of the pubic bone.

3 Gun fa   p 66

Use Gun fa (rolling) on your partner's belly. Work from just below the ribs down to the upper border of the pubic bone, following the meridian pathways. Do this, gently, for 3–4 minutes.

4 Tui fa   p 80

Use Tui fa (pushing) with your palm on the ribcage, working from the end of the sternum round the sides of the body. Do this many times until the ribs feel warm. Work briskly.

5 Yi zhi chan tui fa   p 68

Use one finger meditation on Sp 6 for 3 minutes on both sides, with the movement in the direction of the feet. Then use the same technique on Liv 3 for 3 minutes on both sides, again moving in the direction of the feet.

6 Ca fa   p 76

Ask your partner to turn over so she is lying on her front. Use Ca fa (scrubbing) with the little-finger edge of your hand across the lower back and sacrum. Use some dong qing gao ointment *(see page 56)*.

Treating Qi and blood deficiency

1 Yi zhi chan tui fa   p 68

With your partner lying on her front, use one finger meditation on Bl 20 for 3 minutes on each side. Movement should be directed towards head.

2 Gun fa   p 66

Use rolling technique on your partner's back at the level of the waist on both sides of the spine for about 5 minutes.

3 Ca fa   p 76

Using a little dong qing gao ointment *(see page 56)*, apply scrubbing technique to the sacrum and lower back up to waist level until the area is scorching hot.

Treating stagnation of cold and damp

1 Tui fa p 80

With your partner lying on her back, use Tui fa (pushing) with the palms of your hands on her belly. Work from just below the ribcage down towards the pubic bone. Do this for 3–4 minutes or until the belly feels warm.

2 Mo fa p 72

Use round rubbing on the belly with your palm, first clockwise then anticlockwise, for 5–10 minutes.

3 An rou fa p 89

Use An rou fa (revolving) with your forearm over the navel, first clockwise then anticlockwise, for 3–4 minutes.

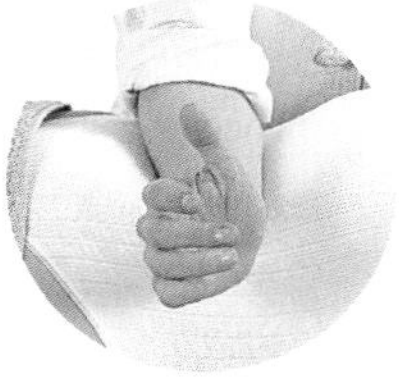

4 Yi zhi chan tui fa p 68

Use one finger meditation on CV 6 and CV 4 for 3 minutes on each point with the movement directed towards the pubic bone.

5 Zhen fa p 84

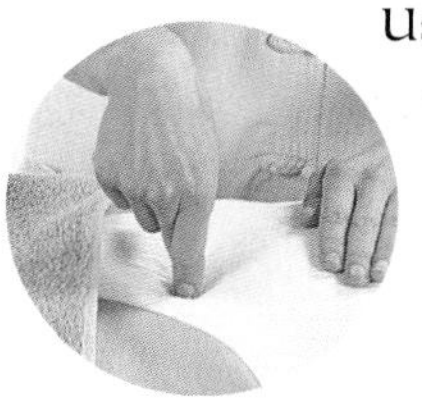

Use Zhen fa (vibrating) on St 29 using your middle finger for 3 minutes.

6 Ji fa p 82

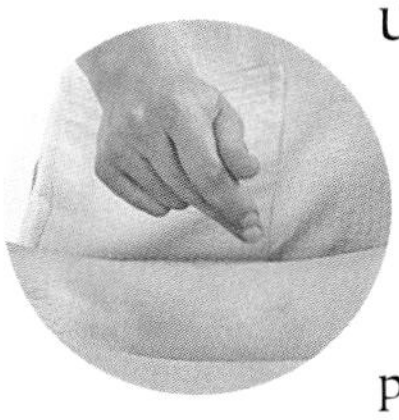

Use Ji fa (dotting) with your middle finger on Sp 6 (*pictured here*) and Sp 8 for 3 minutes on each point on both sides.

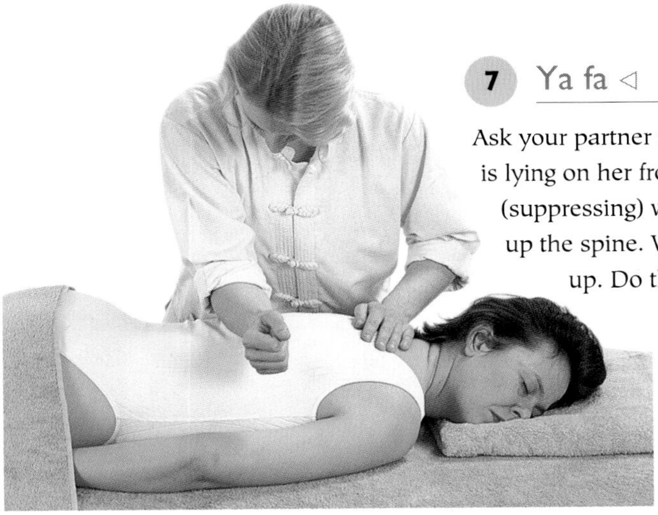

7 Ya fa ◁ p 79

Ask your partner to turn over so she is lying on her front. Use Ya fa (suppressing) with your forearm up the spine. Work from the sacrum up. Do this 3 or 4 times.

8 An rou fa p 89

Use revolving technique with your forearm on the sacrum, first clockwise then anticlockwise, until the sacrum is warm.

9 Ca fa p 76

Apply scrubbing technique using some dong qing gao ointment (*see page 56*) on the spine and either side of the spine until the back is scorching hot.

4 An fa p 78

Ask your partner to turn onto her back. Press with your thumb on St 36 and Sp 6 for 3 minutes on each point, and repeat on the other leg. Concentrate on tonifying while you do this.

5 Mo fa p 72

Use round rubbing on the belly with your palm, first clockwise then anticlockwise, for 5–10 minutes.

6 Zhen fa p 84

Use vibrating technique with your middle finger on CV 4 for 3 minutes. Then vibrate with your whole palm on the belly until it becomes warm.

Diarrhoea

Diarrhoea, the frequent passing of loose or watery stools, can be caused by a variety of factors, both exterior and interior. Tui Na is an extremely valuable form of treatment for this ailment.

Exterior cold, heat, summer heat and damp can invade the body, affecting the stomach, spleen, small intestine and large intestine. Of all the exterior causes of diarrhoea, damp is the most common. It can invade the body via the leg meridians and makes its way to the spleen, blocking it and interfering with its transformation and transportation of food and fluids.

Diet is probably top of the list for causes of diarrhoea. Too much hot- or cold-energy food and food that has gone off or is dirty, frequently cause acute diarrhoea. Eating too much or eating an excessive amount of fatty, raw, greasy or sweet foods can lead to chronic (long-term) diarrhoea. These foods can affect the spleen's transforming and transporting functions – the spleen Qi cannot ascend and rebels downwards causing diarrhoea.

Emotion is another potential cause, as worrying, over-thinking and anger can weaken the spleen. Stress, overworking, lack of rest, over-exercising and excessive sexual activity can weaken the kidney Yang, which then fails to warm the Yang of the spleen, and thus leads to diarrhoea.

Opposite, I have chosen three common patterns of disharmony that are associated with diarrhoea, showing the symptoms and treatment principles for each. Their accompanying Tui Na treatments follow overleaf.

General advice

The spleen is the main organ to consider in cases of diarrhoea. It loathes damp, so steer clear of damp-producing foods, such as dairy products, sweet foods, greasy, oily foods and raw foods. Meditation has a very positive effect on the spleen – it is the opposite of worrying and over-thinking which have a depleting effect on the spleen. In the case of kidney Yang deficiency, rest will probably be crucial; try a few days off work, a walk in natural surroundings and a general easing up on the pace of life. It is good to remember that physical symptoms like diarrhoea are a signal that we are not in balance. By the time a symptom manifests itself physically, the energetic system of the individual will probably have been out of harmony for some time.

Quick point-finder for diarrhoea

You will find the points highlighted here used in the treatment of diarrhoea shown overleaf. These diagrams are a quick reminder *(for exact point location see pages 48–53)*.

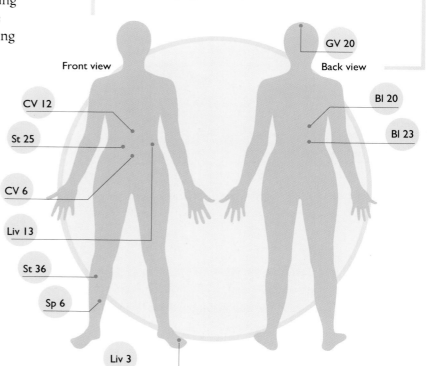

Front view

Back view

GV 20

CV 12

St 25

CV 6

Liv 13

St 36

Sp 6

Liv 3

Bl 20

Bl 23

PATTERN TO BE TREATED: Retention of cold and damp

Causes

Exterior damp and cold invade the spleen, interfering with its function of transforming and transporting.

Signs and symptoms

Diarrhoea may be very watery. Abdominal pain, gurgling in the intestines, a feeling of fullness and bloating in the abdomen, poor appetite, aversion to cold, desire for warmth, feeling of heaviness in the body and limbs. May be accompanied by fever and chills, headache, nasal obstruction.

Tongue

Thick, sticky, greasy white coating

Pulse

Slow and slippery

Treatment principle

Resolve damp, scatter cold, warm middle burner.

Course of treatment

1 treatment per day for 3–5 days; break for 1 day then repeat if necessary.

PATTERN TO BE TREATED: Liver Qi stagnation invading the spleen

Causes

Stress, anxiety, frustration and anger can cause liver Qi to stagnate. The stagnant liver Qi invades the spleen, blocking its transforming and transporting function, causing diarrhoea.

Signs and symptoms

Diarrhoea which can alternate with constipation, bloating in the abdomen, belching, lack of appetite, depression, irritability, tension, feeling of oppression in chest or rib area.

Tongue

Slightly red at the sides, no major changes

Pulse

Wiry, stringy

Treatment principle

Disperse and move liver Qi and tonify the spleen.

Course of treatment

1 treatment per day for 5 days; break for 1 day then repeat as necessary.

PATTERN TO BE TREATED: Kidney Yang deficiency

Causes

Overwork, stress and lack of rest deplete kidney Yang which then cannot warm spleen Yang. There is insufficient warmth for the spleen to function normally and this leads to diarrhoea.

Signs and symptoms

Diarrhoea first thing in the morning. Gurgling in abdomen which stops after bowel movement, cold feeling in abdomen, desire for warmth, weak sore lower back, weak knees.

Tongue

Pale with thin white coating; teeth marks in the sides

Pulse

Deep and weak

Treatment principle

Warm the kidneys and strengthen the spleen.

Course of treatment

1 treatment per day for 5–7 days; 1–2 days' break then repeat as necessary.

Simple treatments for diarrhoea

These treatments cover the patterns of diarrhoea described on the previous two pages. All the techniques are demonstrated in detail in part two and all the points are described in part one. However, as you become more familiar with the techniques, the small pictures here should be enough to guide you. Each technique is shown the first time it appears. As you work, try to concentrate on the relevant treatment principle.

Treating retention of cold and damp

1 Tui fa   p 80

With your partner lying on their back, use Tui fa (pushing) with both palms down the belly, from just below the ribs to the upper border of the pubic bone. Do this until the belly becomes warm.

2 Mo fa   p 72

Use Mo fa (round rubbing) on the abdomen with the palm of one hand. Work first clockwise and then anticlockwise. Do this for 10 minutes in total.

3 An rou fa   p 89

Use An rou fa (revolving) with your forearm on the abdomen just below the navel for 3–5 minutes, working clockwise then anticlockwise.

4 Mo fa   p 72

Use round rubbing with your hands joined over the navel area for 5 minutes, working clockwise.

5 Yi zhi chan tui fa   p 68

Use Yi zhi chan tui fa on CV 12 for 3 minutes with the movement directed towards the pubic bone.

6 An fa and Rou fa ▽ pp 70/78

Use An fa (pressing) combined with Rou fa (kneading) with your thumbs on St 25 for 3 minutes, working both sides at the same time.

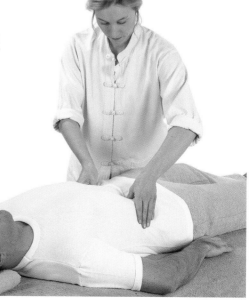

7 Yi zhi chan tui fa   p 68

Use one finger meditation on St 36 for 3 minutes on each leg.

8 Gun fa   p 66

Ask your partner to turn over so they are lying on their front. Use Gun fa (rolling) on the waist area both sides of the spine for 3–4 minutes.

9 Ca fa   p 76

Use Ca fa (scrubbing) on the back both sides of the spine. If you like, use a little toasted sesame oil to help resolve damp. And you could add some ginger juice for its warming properties.

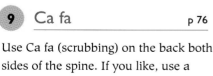

Treating liver Qi stagnation invading the spleen

1 Tui fa p 80

With your partner lying on their back, use pushing technique with the heel of your palm on the chest. Work in lines down the chest following the meridian pathways. Do this repeatedly for about 4 minutes. Then push with your palms on your partner's ribcage. Work both sides simultaneously from the midline down the ribs, until the ribs become warm.

2 Yi zhi chan tui fa p 68

Use one finger meditation on Liv 13 for 3 minutes on both sides.

3 Ji fa p 82

Use Ji fa (dotting) on the chest. Work all over the chest for about 3 minutes.

4 Tui fa p 80

Push with both palms on the abdomen, from just below the ribs to the top of the pubic bone, until the belly is warm.

5 Mo fa p 72

Use round rubbing on the belly with the palm of one hand for 10 minutes; work clockwise then anticlockwise.

6 Pia fa p 90

Use Pia fa (knocking) with your palm over the navel 3 times.

7 Yi zhi chan tui fa p 68

Use one finger meditation on Liv 3 and Sp 6 for 3 minutes on each foot with movement directed towards toes.

8 Cou fa p 75

Stand behind your seated partner and use Cuo fa (rub rolling) over the ribs, from the armpits to the lowest ribs 3 times.

Treating kidney Yang deficiency

1 Mo fa p 72

With your partner lying down on their back, use round rubbing with your palms joined on the abdomen for 10 minutes in a clockwise direction.

2 Zhen fa p 84

Use Zhen fa (vibrating technique) with your palm, first over the navel then on the abdomen, until the belly feels warm.

3 An rou fa p 89

Use revolving with your forearm over the navel area. Work in a clockwise direction for 3–4 minutes.

4 Gun fa p 66

Use rolling technique on the abdomen, towards the ribs, for 3–4 minutes.

5 Zhen fa p 84

Use vibrating technique with your middle finger on CV 6 for 3 minutes.

6 Tui fa p 80

Ask your partner to lie on their front and push with both palms on the back. Work from the shoulders down, along the bladder meridian. You can use dong qing gao ointment (see page 56).

7 Na fa p 74

Use Na fa (grasping) along the bladder meridian. Do this 3–4 times on each side of the spine.

8 An fa and rou fa pp 70/78

Combine pressing and kneading techniques, using your thumbs on Bl 23 and Bl 20 for 3 minutes on each side.

9 Zhen fa p 84

With your partner seated, use vibrating technique with your middle finger on GV 20 for 3 minutes.

Constipation

Constipation refers to the sluggish movement of stools that are infrequent and difficult to pass, often hard in consistency and sometimes dry. There are several possible causes.

Eating too much hot-energy food, such as spices, can dry up body fluids in the stomach and intestines, making stools dry and difficult to move. Too much cold, raw food can interfere with the spleen's transporting function, preventing stools descending. Insufficient fibre is another common cause.

Emotional disharmony and stress are also important factors. Anger, guilt, resentment and frustration can, over time, stagnate liver Qi and prevent it flowing freely in the intestines. In some individuals, worry, anxiety and over-thinking weaken spleen Qi, making its ability to transport food sluggish. Not getting enough exercise is another common cause, particularly in the West. This can weaken spleen Qi and cause stagnation of liver Qi.

Working too hard for a long period of time and not relaxing enough may weaken the kidneys. If kidney Yin becomes weak, the stools can get dry; if kidney Yang becomes deficient, it can lead to internal cold which contracts the intestines, causing constipation.

In terms of exterior pathogens, heat is the most likely cause of constipation. If an attack of wind heat is not cleared, it can move deeper into the body affecting the lungs, stomach and intestines. In this case, there would be very strong symptoms of heat, such as high fever, sweating, thirst, a red tongue and rapid pulse. The intense heat soon dries the body fluids and therefore the stools.

Tui Na is highly effective in treating constipation and can have very fast results. Below and opposite are three common patterns of disharmony; their step-by-step treatments are shown overleaf.

General advice

If you or someone you are treating has constipation, it is best to avoid taking laxatives which can, in the long run, make the problem worse and more difficult to treat. In the case of liver Qi stagnation, regular exercise will help, as will meditation to calm the mind. With deep underlying emotional causes leading to stagnation, the roots of the issues will need to be worked through to prevent the symptom returning. In the case of Qi deficiency, rest and a regular balanced diet are essential, and Qi Gong exercises will help to build up Qi. Where heat is the cause, it is important to cut out all hot-energy foods (spices, curries, alcohol and red meat).

In order to help evacuation in general, it is worth trying this simple exercise when you are trying to pass stools. First, relax as much as possible. Breathe deeply and imagine you are breathing into your sacrum area. Then stimulate LI 4 with Rou fa *(see pages 70–71)*. Do this on both hands for a couple of minutes – it can be quite effective.

PATTERN TO BE TREATED: Stagnation of liver Qi

Causes	Signs and symptoms		Treatment principle	Course of treatment
The liver controls the smooth flow of Qi throughout the entire body. If liver Qi stagnates in the large intestine, the stools become all bound up and cannot move and descend.	Desire to pass stools but difficulty and straining to pass small compacted, but not dry, stools (like sheep's droppings). Abdominal bloating, flatulence, a full feeling in the epigastrium and/or rib area, irritability, belching.		Calm the liver, disperse stagnation, encourage Qi to descend.	1 treatment per day for 3 days; a break for 1 day then repeat as necessary.
	Tongue	*Pulse*		
	No change, or a little red at the sides	Wiry		

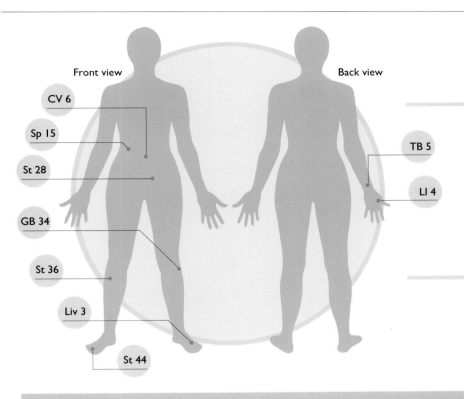

Front view

Back view

CV 6

Sp 15

St 28

GB 34

St 36

Liv 3

St 44

TB 5

LI 4

Quick point-finder for constipation

You will find the points highlighted here used in the treatment of constipation shown overleaf. These diagrams are a quick reminder *(for exact point location see pages 48–53).*

PATTERN TO BE TREATED: Accumulation of heat in the stomach and intestines

Causes	Signs and symptoms		Treatment principle	Course of treatment
Interior heat dries up the body fluids and stools making them difficult to pass.	Dry hard stools, no bowel movements for several days, thirst, red face, scanty dark urine, abdominal pain which is worse with pressure, feeling of heat, smelly breath.		Clear the heat, moisten the intestines.	1 treatment per day for 5 days; a break of 2 days then repeat as necessary.
	Tongue Red with yellow greasy coating; red points around the centre and back of tongue	*Pulse* Rapid and slippery		

PATTERN TO BE TREATED: Constipation from Qi deficiency

Causes	Signs and symptoms		Treatment principle	Course of treatment
Spleen and/or lung Qi become deficient. If spleen Qi is weak, it cannot move stools. If lung Qi is weak, it cannot send Qi to the large intestine (its Yang organ partner) and there is not enough Qi for evacuation.	Desire to pass stools but much straining and effort required. Infrequent evacuation, a feeling of weakness and exhaustion after evacuation, stools are thin and long but not dry, shortness of breath, pale complexion, tiredness.		Tonify Qi, relax the intestines.	1 treatment per day for 5 days; break of 1 day then repeat as necessary.
	Tongue Pale	*Pulse* Weak, feeble		

Simple treatments for constipation

These treatments cover the patterns of constipation described on the previous two pages. All the techniques are demonstrated in detail in part two and all the points are described in part one. However, as you become more familiar with the techniques, the small pictures here should be enough to guide you. Each technique is shown the first time it appears. As you work, try to concentrate on the relevant treatment principle.

Treating stagnation of liver Qi

1 Tui fa p 80

With your partner lying on their back, use Tui fa (pushing) with the palms of both your hands on the belly, working from just below the ribs downwards to just above the top of the pubic bone. Work briskly for 3–4 minutes or until the belly feels warm.

2 Mo fa p 72

Use Mo fa (round rubbing) on the belly using the palm of one hand. Work briskly in an anticlockwise direction for 5 minutes.

3 Gun fa p 66

Use Gun fa (rolling) all over the belly. Work from just below the ribs downwards to just above the pubic bone, following the meridian pathways. Continue like this for 5 minutes.

4 Yi zhi chan tui fa p 68

Use Yi zhi chan tui fa (one finger meditation) on CV 6 for 3 minutes, with the movement directed towards the feet. Work quite vigorously on this point.

5 Pia fa p 90

Use Pia fa (knocking) with your fingertips all over the belly, working in anticlockwise circles and in lines following the meridian pathways. Do this for about 3 minutes.

6 Zhen fa p 84

Use Zhen fa (vibrating) with your palm over the navel, either side of the navel and below the navel, for about 2 minutes on each area.

7 Yi zhi chan tui fa p 68

Use one finger meditation on Sp 15, working towards the feet. Use the same technique to on Liv 3, with movement directed towards the toes. Then stimulate GB 34, with movement directed towards the head. Work on each point, on both sides, for 3 minutes.

8 Cuo fa ◁ p 75

Ask your partner to sit up. Stand behind them and use Cuo fa (rub rolling) on the flanks, working from just below the armpits to the bottom of the ribs. Do this 3 times.

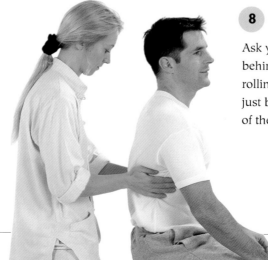

Treating accumulation of heat in the stomach and intestines

1   Na fa   p 74

With your partner lying on their front, use Na fa (grasping) along the bladder meridian where the transporting points lie *(see page 50)*. Work briskly from the nape down to the sacrum on both sides of the spine, grasping, lifting then releasing. Do this 5 times on each side of the spine.

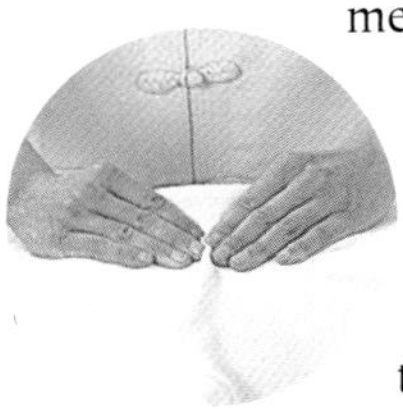

2   Tui fa   p 80

Use pushing technique with both palms down the back from nape to sacrum for 3–4 minutes.

4   Che fa   p 92

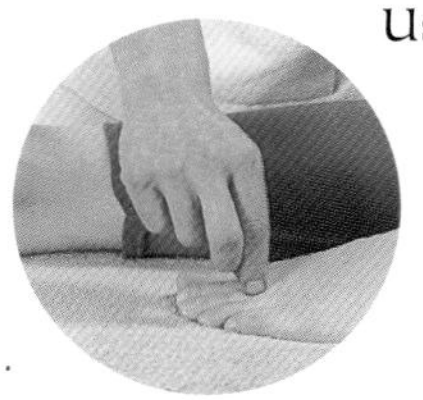

Use Che fa (tweaking technique) on LI 4 and St 44 *(pictured here)* for 3 minutes on each foot.

3   Yi zhi chan tui fa   p 68

Ask your partner to turn onto their back. Use Yi zhi chan tui fa on TB 5 for 3 minutes on both sides, moving towards your partner's hands.

5   Gun fa   p 66

Use rolling technique on the belly, following the meridian pathways from just below the ribs to just above the pubic bone. Work briskly for 5 minutes.

6   Pia fa   p 90

Use knocking technique with your fingertips on the belly in anticlockwise circles and in lines following the meridian pathways for 3 minutes.

7   Zhen fa   p 84

Vibrate with the palm of your hand on the navel, either side of the navel and below the navel for 2 minutes on each area.

8   Yi zhi chan tui fa   p 68

Use one finger meditation on St 28 on the left side only for 3 minutes, working vigorously with the movement directed towards the head.

Treating Qi deficiency

1   Tui fa   p 80

With your partner lying on their back, use pushing technique on the chest with the heel of your palm. Work in lines that follow the meridian pathways all over the chest area, pushing down from the collar bone for 3 minutes.

2   An fa and Rou fa ▷   pp 70/78

Use An fa (pressing) combined with Rou fa (kneading) with the heel of your palm or your thumb on the chest. Follow the lines of the meridian pathways downwards from the collar bone for 3 minutes.

3   Zhen fa   p 84

Apply vibrating technique with your finger on CV 6 for 3 minutes.

6   Zhen fa   p 84

Apply vibrating technique on Sp 15 on both sides for 3 minutes.

7   Na fa   p 74

Use grasping technique all over the abdomen, working gently for 3 minutes.

4   Rou fa   p 70

Use kneading technique on the abdomen gently with the heel of your palm or your whole palm *(pictured here)*, working in clockwise circles for 3–4 minutes.

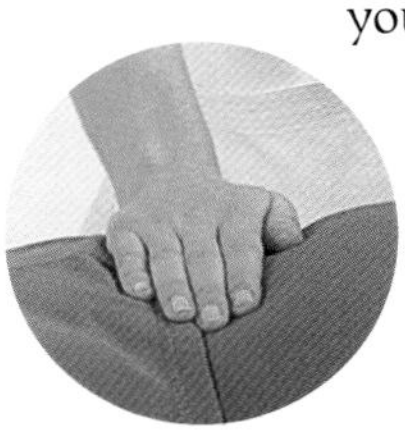

5   Mo fa   p 72

Use round rubbing with joined palms on the abdomen in a clockwise direction for 5 minutes.

8   Yi zhi chan tui fa   p 68

Use one finger meditation on St 36 for 3 minutes on both sides, with the movement directed towards your partner's feet. You can use toasted sesame oil directly on the skin for this treatment – it has a tonifying effect.

Epigastric Pain

Epigastric pain is stomach ache anywhere between the sternum and the navel, sometimes moving to the lower rib region.

Eating habits are the major cause of epigastric pain. Eating too much can lead to retention of food, which prevents stomach Qi descending. Eating too little depletes stomach and spleen Qi. Eating too many cold foods, such as salads and ice cream, can create interior cold in the stomach and spleen. Too many hot foods, like spices and alcohol, can create stomach heat.

Irregular eating habits, like skipping a meal one day then eating a huge meal the next, will also weaken stomach Qi. Eating whilst reading or watching television can stagnate stomach Qi, leading to retention of food.

Constantly skipping breakfast can lead to stomach Qi deficiency and blood deficiency. The stomach's main hours of activity are between 7 and 9 am, hence the saying, 'Breakfast like a king, lunch like a prince and dine like a pauper.'

Emotions can have a profound effect on digestion. Anger, worry and anxiety can cause Qi to stagnate, leading to retention of food. Other causes of epigastric pain are overexertion, working too hard and invasions of exterior pathogens, such as cold, damp and heat.

Tui Na is tremendously beneficial in many cases of epigastric pain. The tables below outline the symptoms and the treatment principles for three common patterns. Overleaf are the step-by-step treatments for each.

PATTERN TO BE TREATED: Retention of food

Causes	Signs and symptoms		Treatment principle	Course of treatment
Over eating or weak stomach Qi leads to a build-up of undigested food in the stomach.	Dull epigastric pain which is made worse with the application of pressure. Bloated, full feeling, belching, acidic regurgitation, smelly breath, nausea, vomiting, pain relieved by vomiting, loose stools or constipation, dislike the smell of food.		Promote digestion, dissolve food accumulation, move stagnation.	1 treatment per day for 10 days; a break of 5 days then repeat as necessary.
	Tongue Thick, greasy coating	*Pulse* Slippery		

PATTERN TO BE TREATED: Epigastric pain from stagnation of Qi

Causes	Signs and symptoms		Treatment principle	Course of treatment
Stagnant liver Qi invades the stomach and prevents the normal descending of stomach Qi. In terms of the five elements, wood overacts upon earth. This pattern is mostly due to emotions like anger and frustration.	Epigastric pain and bloating. The pain moves to right or left rib area. Belching, a full feeling in the chest, frequent sighing, irritability, pain is clearly made worse when the individual is stressed, a feeling of hunger.		Calm the liver, move stagnant Qi.	1 treatment for 10 days; a break of 5 days then repeat as necessary.
	Tongue No changes, or somewhat red at sides	*Pulse* Stringy, wiry, particularly on the left-hand side		

General advice

If you or the person you are treating suffers with epigastric pain, it is important to begin to balance dietary habits – but too much change too quickly is not always the best approach. I generally advise my patients to introduce changes gradually, cutting down bit by bit on the foods that may be creating cold, heat or damp in their bodies and gently adopting healthier eating patterns. If someone is used to skipping breakfast, it is good to encourage them to start with something small in the morning. If they have a stomach and spleen deficiency and have no appetite in the morning, a cup of ginger tea will help to warm the stomach and, in a few weeks, their appetite will begin to improve. All you need for ginger tea is a couple of slices of fresh root ginger. Boil them in a pan with enough water for your cup. Let it simmer for 2–3 minutes, then discard the ginger slices and drink the fluid.

It is also important to take time to eat. Sit down and leave passionate conversations and work until later. A gentle stroll after eating is very beneficial, and dropping the habit of reading the paper or watching TV while eating will go a long way to improving the energetic balance of your digestive system. Research has shown that the vast majority of people with stomach ulcers habitually read the paper whilst eating.

Quick point-finder for epigastric pain

You will find the points highlighted here used in the treatment of epigastric pain shown overleaf. These diagrams are a quick reminder *(for exact point location see pages 48–53).*

Front view
Back view

CV 13
CV 12
P 6
GB 34
St 36
Sp 4
St 44
BI 20
BI 21

PATTERN TO BE TREATED: Epigastric pain from a cold deficient stomach and spleen

Causes	Signs and symptoms		Treatment principle	Course of treatment
Spleen and stomach Qi have become weak. Yang is deficient and produces an interior deficient cold pattern.	Dull epigastric pain which is made better if the belly is pressed and after eating and with the application of heat. Poor appetite, vomiting clear watery fluids, tiredness, loose stools, cold limbs, general chilliness, pale complexion.		Warm the middle burner, strengthen the stomach and spleen.	1 treatment per day for 10 days; 5 days' break then repeat as necessary.
	Tongue	*Pulse*		
	Pale with thin white coating	Deep, weak		

Simple treatments for epigastric pain

These treatments cover the patterns of epigastric pain described on the previous two pages. All the techniques are demonstrated in detail in part two and all the points are described in part one. However, as you become more familiar with the techniques, the small pictures here should be enough to guide you. Each technique is shown the first time it appears. As you work, try to concentrate on the relevant treatment principle.

Treating retention of food

1 Ji fa   p 82

With your partner lying on their front, use Ji fa (chopping) with your palms first separated and then joined all over the back, buttocks and legs. Work briskly for 4 minutes up and down the body.

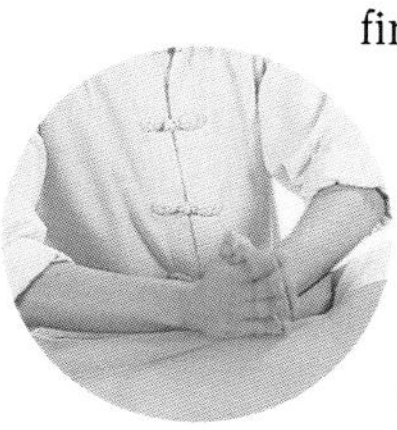

2 Pia fa   p 90

Use Pia fa (knocking) all over the back, buttocks and legs using a hollow palm for 2 minutes.

3 Tui fa   p 80

Ask your partner to turn onto their back. Use Tui fa (pushing) with both palms on the belly, working from just below the ribs down to the upper border of the pubic bone. Work quickly for 3–4 minutes, imagining the food moving downwards.

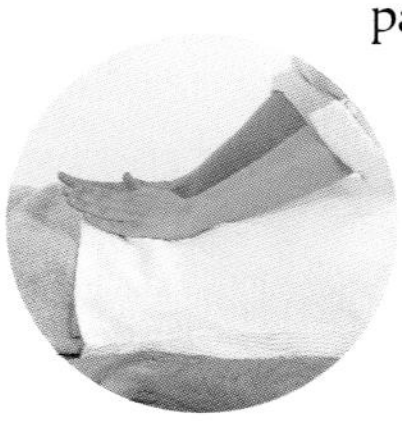

4 Mo fa   p 72

Use Mo fa (round rubbing) on the belly, working in an anticlockwise direction with the palm of one hand for 5 minutes.

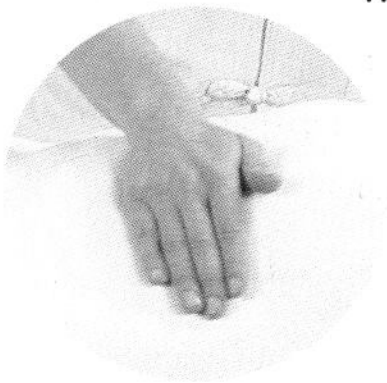

5 An rou fa   p 89

Use An rou fa (revolving) with your forearm just below the navel, working anticlockwise for 3–4 minutes.

6 Gun fa   p 66

Use Gun fa (rolling) all over the belly, working in lines following the meridian pathways for 3–4 minutes.

7 Zhen fa   p 84

Use Zhen fa (vibrating) with your middle finger on CV 13 for 3 minutes.

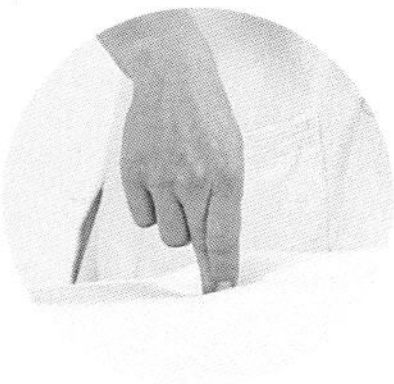

8 Yi zhi chan tui fa   p 68

Use Yi zhi chan tui fa (one finger meditation) on Sp 4 and P 6 (pictured here) for 3 minutes on each point on both sides.

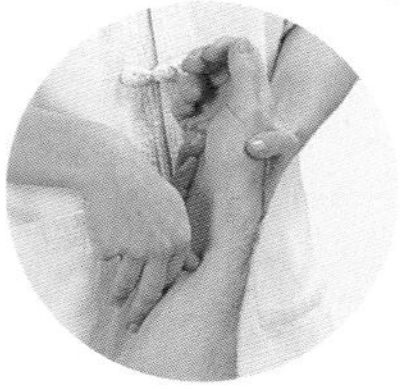

9 Che fa   p 92

Use Che fa (tweaking technique) with the tips of your thumb and index finger on St 44.

Treating stagnation Of Qi

1 An rou fa p 89

With your partner lying on their back, use revolving technique with your forearm just above the navel for 3 minutes in an anticlockwise direction.

2 Ji fa p 82

Use chopping technique with your palms joined all over the legs and arms for 3–4 minutes.

3 Zhen fa p 84

Use vibrating technique on CV 12 for 3 minutes with the tip of your finger.

4 Gun fa p 66

Use rolling technique on the belly for 3–4 minutes, working in lines following the meridian pathways.

5 Mo fa p 72

Use round rubbing on the belly with the palm of your hand, working in anticlockwise circles for 5 minutes.

6 Pia fa p 90

Use knocking technique on the belly with your fingertips. Work in anticlockwise circles or in lines following the meridian pathways for 3–4 minutes.

7 Yi zhi chan tui fa p 68

Use one finger meditation on St 36, P 6 and GB 34 for 3 minutes on each point on both sides of the body.

8 Ji fa p 82

Ask your partner to turn onto their front and use chopping technique with the back of the hand all over the back, buttocks and legs for 3–4 minutes.

Treating a cold deficient stomach and spleen

1 Yi zhi chan tui fa p 68

With your partner lying on their front, use one finger meditation on Bl 20 and Bl 21 for 3 minutes on each point on both sides, with the movement directed towards your partner's feet.

2 Ca fa p 76

Use Ca fa (scrubbing) on the bladder meridian either side of the spine until the back feels scorching hot. Use a little don qing gao ointment (see page 56) for this.

3 Tui fa p 80

Ask your partner to turn over so they are lying on their back. Apply pushing technique on the belly using a little toasted sesame oil. Work from just below the ribs downwards to the upper border of the pubic bone for 3–4 minutes.

4 Mo fa p 72

Use round rubbing with joined palms on the belly, working in clockwise circles for 5 minutes.

5 An fa and Rou fa pp 70/78

Use An fa (pressing) combined with Rou fa (kneading) using the palm of your hand on the belly, working slowly and gently in clockwise circles for 3 minutes.

6 Gun fa p 66

Use rolling technique on both arms for about 2 minutes on each arm.

7 Zhen fa p 84

Use vibrating technique with your middle finger on CV 12 for 3 minutes.

8 Yi zhi chan tui fa p 68

Use one finger meditation on St 36 for 3 minutes on each leg.

Bi Syndrome

Musculoskeletal conditions – such as tennis elbow, wryneck, frozen shoulder, lower back ache, sciatica, arthritis and rheumatism – come under the category of what is known in Chinese medicine as 'Bi Syndrome'. 'Bi' means obstruction and, as the old Chinese saying states, 'Where there is obstruction there is pain'.

Case history

Name   Benjamin

Age   40 years

Symptoms and diagnosis

Benjamin came to see me with a frozen shoulder. There were symptoms of stiffness and pain in the shoulder joint and surrounding muscles and pain in several other joints in the body, indicating the presence of pathogenic wind. There was swelling in the joint and a feeling of heaviness in the area, with symptoms becoming worse when the weather was cloudy, rainy and damp – indicating the presence of pathogenic damp – and better for the application of heat – indicating the presence of pathogenic cold.

Diagnosis

An invasion of wind damp cold, with damp dominant.

Treatment

The treatment involved expelling wind, resolving damp and scattering or warming cold. Particular points were chosen for this purpose and to strengthen the individual's defensive Qi to help prevent further attacks. Tui Na techniques were chosen to remove obstructions from the affected meridians and local area and to increase the flow of Qi and blood.

Tui Na is renowned for its highly effective treatment of musculoskeletal conditions. In hospitals in China the Tui Na departments are without a doubt the first port of call for all problems of this nature. Whilst working at the hospital of traditional Chinese medicine in Nanjing, from 8am onwards, I treated one patient after another as they queued up for treatments of both acute traumatic injuries and chronic musculoskeletal disorders. By the end of the first week we students were exhausted. Fortunately, with the support and encouragement of our teachers, we soon became accustomed to the schedule.

In the West, Tui Na is still in its infancy and people are just beginning to discover the benefits of this form of treatment. In my practice, I treat many people who have already trodden the paths of physiotherapy, chiropractic and osteopathy. Their musculoskeletal problems have been hanging around for months and often even years. Tui Na consistently comes up with excellent results, totally clearing or, at the very least, producing a lasting reduction in both acute and chronic pain, and frequently in a surprisingly short time. The approach of Tui Na is holistic and it offers many benefits to the overall health of an individual as well as relief from pain.

In Chinese medicine terms, there are various causes that can lead to Bi Syndrome. The meridians can be invaded by exterior pathogenic factors which obstruct the flow of Qi and blood. Wind has a tendency to drive cold, heat or damp with it into the body. In fact, we can say that Bi Syndrome of this nature can be categorized as either an invasion of wind damp heat or wind damp cold. Usually one pathogen in either of these cases will be dominant. The table opposite gives the symptoms associated with each pathogen in the case of Bi Syndrome.

Over the next eleven pages you will find simple Tui Na treatments for tennis elbow, stiff neck, low back pain and sciatica. These are all very common complaints that a Tui Na practitioner would treat on a regular basis.

How external pathogens manifest in Bi Syndrome

Wind Predominates	Signs and symptoms	Damp Predominates	Signs and symptoms
This is known as 'Wandering Bi'	Rapid onset of symptoms Rapid change in symptoms Pain that moves location Pain that involves several joints Aversion to wind Stiffness and pain in muscles and joints Possibly also fever, chills and other symptoms of an exterior invasion (such as floating, superficial pulse)	This is known as 'Fixed Bi'	Pain in muscles and joints with a fixed location Heaviness in the affected area, a feeling that the area is tightly bound Stiffness and numbness more than pain Swelling Worse on cloudy, rainy, damp days Often affects the lower parts of the body Thick, greasy tongue coating Slippery, soggy pulse
Cold Predominates	Signs and symptoms	Heat Predominates	Signs and symptoms
This is known as 'Painful Bi'	Signs of contraction and stagnation Severe biting or stabbing pain Worse for cold and better for warmth No redness or feelings of heat Thin sticky white tongue coating Tight, stringy, wiry pulse	This is known as 'Hot Bi'	Redness Hot to touch Pain that is so bad the person cannot bear to be touched Rapid pulse Red tongue with yellow coating Possibly also other heat signs (such as thirst, fever, irritability)

Other causes of Bi Syndrome

Traumatic injury	This creates blood stasis which obstructs the flow of Qi and blood.	Interior disharmony	For example, if the spleen becomes weak from a poor diet and excessive worrying, damp may be formed in the spleen. If at the same time the liver has become hot from feelings of anger, damp and heat can combine creating 'Hot Bi', as is seen in various musculoskeletal conditions, such as rheumatoid arthritis.
Overstrain	This damages the muscles and over time may weaken the spleen, as the spleen governs the muscles.		
Lack of exercise	This causes Qi and blood to stagnate. Physical movement and exercise promote the circulation of blood and Qi.		

Tennis elbow

This condition is usually due to overuse and is not always sports-related. Repetitive activities that involve twisting the forearm, such as using a screwdriver, often create this kind of strain. The pain and soreness are generally felt at the back and on the outside of the elbow joint. Sometimes there is swelling, too. Movement is restricted and the pain often affects the muscles that extend the forearm. The upper arm and shoulder can also be affected. The patient concerned will probably find it difficult to rotate their arm and to hold and carry things. Tennis elbow is usually related to the large intestine meridian, but I have often seen this condition affecting all three Yang meridians of the arm (large intestine, small intestine and triple burner). The most important factors in tennis elbow are blood stasis and stagnation of Qi in the meridians, muscles, tendons and elbow joint.

Treatment principle

Promote the flow of Qi and blood, soften the tendons, clear the affected meridians, eliminate stasis and relieve spasm and pain.

Course of treatment

1 treatment per day for 10 days. Break treatment for 2 days, then repeat the course.

Treating tennis elbow

1 Yi zhi chan tui fa   p 68

With your partner seated, use Yi zhi chan tui fa (one finger meditation) on LI 11 for 3 minutes. Direct the movement of the technique towards his hand.

2 Yi zhi chan tui fa   p 68

Use one finger meditation on LI 10, TB 5 and LI 4 for 3 minutes on each point. As before, have your partner seated and direct the movement towards your partner's hand.

3 Gun fa   p 66

Stand at your patient's side and hold the affected arm just above the wrist. Bring the arm out to the side so that it is in front of you. Using your other hand, apply Gun fa (rolling), working from the shoulder down the arm to the wrist. Continue for about 10 minutes.

6 Cuo fa   p 75

Use Cuo fa (rub rolling), working from your partner's shoulder down his arm to the hand. Pay a little extra attention to the elbow joint when you get there. Do this technique 3 or 4 times.

7 Dou fa   p 85

Use Dou fa (shaking), holding your partner's arm with both of your hands just above their wrist. Ask your partner to keep his body weight centred so you can use a little traction on his arm. Do this for 2–3 minutes.

8 Nian fa   p 93

Use Nian fa (holding twisting) on the fingers and thumb of your partner. Apply the technique to the thumb and each finger twice.

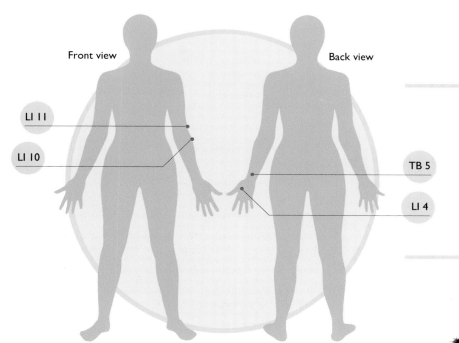

Front view

Back view

LI 11

LI 10

TB 5

LI 4

Quick point-finder for tennis elbow

You will find the points highlighted here used in the treatment of tennis elbow given below. These diagrams serve as a quick reminder *(for exact point location see pages 48–53).*

4   Na fa   p 74

Use Na fa (grasping) down the three Yang and three Yin meridians of the arm, working from the shoulder to wrist. Do this repeatedly for 4 minutes or until the arm feels warm.

5   Na fa and Che fa ▷ pp 74/92

Use grasping technique again, but this time combined with Che fa (nipping). Apply this on the elbow joint for 3–4 minutes.

9   Ca fa   p 76

Using a little don qing gao ointment *(see page 56),* use Ca fa (scrubbing) with the heel of your palm on your partner's elbow joint and over the extensor muscles at the front of the forearm. Continue until the whole area feels scorching hot.

10   Dou fa   p 85

Once again, use shaking technique. Shake the affected arm 3 times, but adjust the technique slightly this time by adding a short, sharp jerking movement at the end of each shake.

Further treatment

The Qi Gong clearing exercise on page 58 can be useful in cases of tennis elbow. If you teach your patient to stimulate the points you have used during the treatment with Rou Fa (kneading) it will improve their rate of recovery. Advise your patient not to use ice on their elbow: it will lead to more blood stasis and Qi stagnation.

Stiff Neck

Stiffness of the neck (or wryneck) is a common condition ranging from mild to severe. The symptoms are pain, stiffness and spasm, usually on one side only of the sternocleidomastiod and trapezius muscles (see page 45). The head inclines towards the affected side and the sufferer experiences restriction of movement, with great difficulty in turning their head from side to side. In severe cases, the muscles of the upper back and shoulders can also be affected, and the pain can be very debilitating.

The symptoms usually occur on waking up after a night's sleep, generally due to sleeping in an awkward position or with the pillows too high, or being exposed to a draught whilst sleeping. A stiff neck can also be due to spraining the neck muscles by turning the head too quickly.

In traditional Chinese medicine terms, a stiff neck is associated with stagnation of Qi and blood or, in cases caused by exposure to a draught, an invasion of wind cold.

Tui Na will usually sort things out in 2 treatments, unless the problem is very severe or has come on top of an already existing long-term neck problem, in which case more sessions will be necessary. Below is a simple step-by-step treatment for wryneck caused by stagnation of Qi and blood.

Treating stiff neck

1   Yi zhi chan tui fa ▽   p 68

With your partner seated, use Yi zhi chan tui fa (one finger meditation) on GB 20 (pictured here) and GB 21 for 3 minutes on both points. You can just stimulate these points on the affected side only, but for balance I tend to stimulate the points on both sides.

2   Gun fa   p 66

Stand by the affected side of your partner and use Gun fa (rolling) on the affected side all over the top of the shoulder and the side and back of the neck. Do this for 10 minutes then do the same on the other side of the body to balance things out.

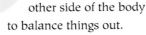

3   An fa and Rou fa   pp 70/78

Using your thumb, apply An fa (pressing) in combination with Rou fa (kneading). Work first between each of the cervical vertebrae of the neck along the governing vessel meridian, then just to one side of the vertebrae and down the bladder and gall bladder meridians of the neck. Work 3 times on each meridian on both sides.

5   Yao fa   p 86

Use Yao fa (rotation) on the neck, working first towards the affected side then away from the affected side. Start gently with small rotations and gradually make the movement stronger and larger.

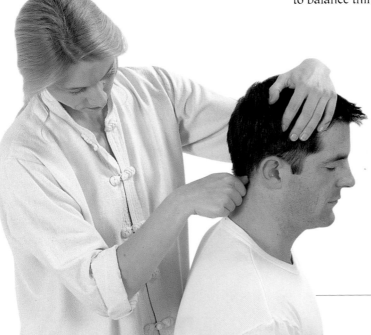

Treatment principle

Relax the tendons and muscles, invigorate the flow of Qi and blood, ease pain and spasm.

Course of treatment

Up to 3 treatments on consecutive days is usually sufficient.

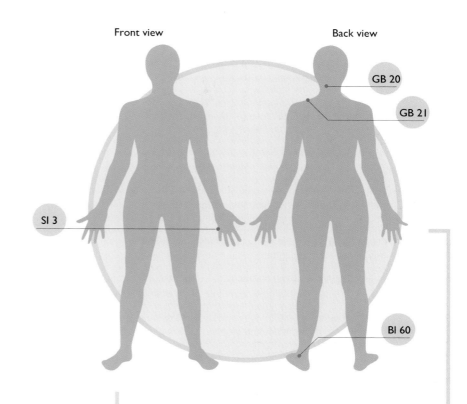

Front view   Back view

GB 20

GB 21

SI 3

Bl 60

Quick point-finder for stiff neck

You will find the points highlighted here used in the treatment of stiff neck shown here. These diagrams are a quick reminder *(for exact point location see pages 48–53).*

---

4 Na fa   p 74

Use Na fa (grasping) on the neck, working from the base of the skull down to the nape *(pictured here)*. Do

this for 3–4 minutes or until the neck feels warm. Then apply the technique on the top of both shoulders at the same time. Grasp, lift the muscle and quickly release it. Do this briskly for 2–3 minutes.

---

6 Ban shen fa   p 88

Use Ban shen fa (pulling) on the neck. Hold the base of your partner's skull with both hands and gently and gradually pull their head upwards, creating traction on their neck. Do this 3 times.

---

7 Yi zhi chan tui fa   p 68

Use one finger meditation on SI 3 and Bl 60 for 3 minutes on each point on both sides of the body.

Further treatment

Ask your patient to stimulate SI 3 and Bl 60 themselves by kneading or nipping several times a day. In terms of sleeping positions, it is always best to lie on the right side with your left arm resting on your left leg and right arm bent in front of you. Tuck your chin in slightly to straighten your neck. Try to avoid sleeping next to a window.

Low Back Pain

Every week I see case after case of lower back problems, from nagging dull aches to severe disabling pain. More days are taken off work for this complaint than any other.

One patient of mine, a woman in her late twenties, had already taken four months off work before she came to see me. She worked with nursery school children and was constantly having to bend down to lift and carry the little ones. She was also forced to sit on chairs made for five year olds as there were no other chairs available. Over a period of time, this led to chronic overstrain of her lumbar muscles and sciatica. She came for treatment once a week for 2 months and is now pain free and back at work. Tui Na is really at its best with this ailment. I have seen amazing results even with the most stubborn cases, both in China and in my own practice.

Low back pain is felt anywhere from the lower ribs to the crease below the buttocks. There are several causes, but the meridians affected are usually the bladder, kidney, gall bladder and governing vessel.

Causes of low back pain

Excessive physical work is a common cause of lower back problems. I see many dancers, gardeners, builders, carpenters and sportspeople whose jobs can put a great strain on their back muscles and on their kidney Qi, which energetically can become weak from the daily physical demands put upon their bodies.

On a par with cases of lower back ache due to excessive physical work are those due to lack of exercise. Many of my patients have jobs that involve sitting down at a computer all day or driving long distances. Lack of physical movement combined with poor posture leads to a weakening of the joints of the spine and their supporting ligaments. Disc problems are often due to these factors. Another cause is invasion of the back muscles by exterior damp and cold. This can lead to acute or chronic back ache. Excessive sexual activity can also be a factor in chronic cases, leading to a weakening of kidney Qi, which then fails to support and strengthen the back muscles.

For women, a common cause is pregnancy and childbirth. Once again, the back muscles can become strained and the kidney Qi depleted as the kidney energy has further demands put upon it during this time. Sciatica is common in the last trimester of pregnancy because, as the baby prepares to engage, pressure is placed on the mother's nerves in the lower back.

In Chinese medicine the most important factors in lower back ache are stagnation of Qi

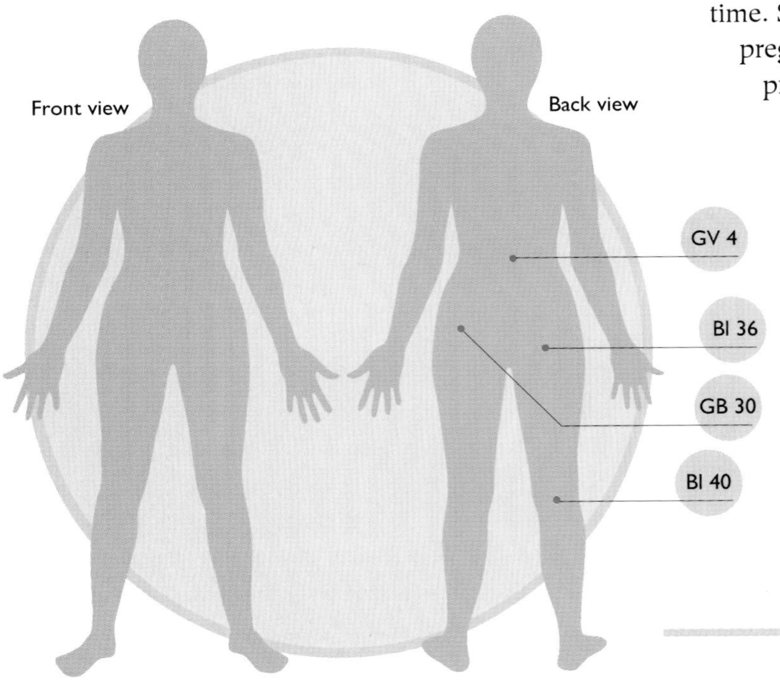

Front view

Back view

GV 4

Bl 36

GB 30

Bl 40

Quick point-finder for low back pain

You will find the points highlighted here used in the treatment of low back pain shown here. These diagrams are a quick reminder (for exact point location see pages 48–53).

and blood, retention of cold and damp and kidney Qi deficiency. The following treatment is for low back pain caused by overstrain of the lumber muscles leading to stagnation of Qi and blood. The symptoms are strong stabbing pains to one or both sides of the lumber spine, often worse in the morning after sleep and better as the day goes on. It will generally be better for a little light exercise, such as walking, and worse for sitting or standing for any length of time. The back muscles are stiff and rigid and the sufferer will find it difficult to bend and turn from the waist.

General advice

An important factor to remember with back problems is posture or correct use of the body. I recommend the Alexander Technique: it is a wonderful method of rediscovering the easy natural way we all once used our bodies when we were small children, and to release muscular tension. There are many Alexander Technique teachers now who teach both on a one to one basis and in a class situation.

Treatment principle

Relax the tendons and muscles, invigorate the flow of Qi and blood, ease pain and spasm.

Course of treatment

1 treatment 3 times per week for 3–4 weeks.

Back exercises

There are several gentle exercises I teach to my patients with low back pain to help keep the Qi and blood moving between treatments and to aid recovery. Here are three exercises you may find useful yourself, as well as teaching them to someone you are treating. They have the benefit of keeping the back in good shape and, therefore, preventing lower back problems from reoccurring or indeed manifesting in the first place.

Massaging exercise

Lie down on your back on a firm surface – a carpeted floor is ideal. Bring your knees up to your chest and hold your knees with your hands. Then, using the strength of your arms, circle your legs, first in one direction for 3–4 minutes then in the opposite direction. This has the effect of massaging your lower back against the floor. This exercise is not strenuous and people generally find it comforting and relieving.

'Hedgehog roll' exercise

Start by lying on your back as in the previous exercise then start rocking gently backwards and forwards. When you roll backwards breathe in and when you roll forwards breathe out.

Gradually make the rolling movement bigger so that when you roll forwards you sit up and when you roll backwards your toes touch behind your head. Do not try to force it – just go as far as you comfortably can.

Stretching exercise

Lie on your back with your feet flat on the floor and your knees pointing up towards the ceiling. Now cross your right leg over your left and spread both your arms out to the sides. Turn your head to the right and let your legs drop down to the left. This creates a wonderful gentle twisting stretch for your back. You can increase the stretch by pressing down gently on your right knee. Do exactly the same on the other side.

Treating overstrained lumbar muscles

1 Gun fa   p 66

With your partner lying on their front, use Gun fa (rolling) from the waist area down the lumbar muscles either side  of the spine, over the sacrum and buttocks, and down the backs of the legs. Do this repeatedly for 20 minutes.

2 An fa and Rou fa ▷ pp 70/78

Use Rou fa (kneading) with the heel of the palm of one hand on the lumbar muscles. At the same time, use An fa (pressing) with the thumb of your other hand down the bladder meridian on the calf. Do this for about 5 minutes on each side.

3 An rou fa   p 89

Use An rou fa (revolving) with your forearm from your partner's waist all the way down the lumbar muscles  across the spine and on the buttocks. Do this for about 5 minutes or until the muscles feel warm.

4 Na fa   p 74

Use Na fa (grasping) with both of your hands on the lumbar muscles from the waist down, grasping the muscles on either side of the spine simultaneously. Do this for 2–3 minutes.

5 Ban shen fa   p 88

Use Ban shen fa (pulling). Press one palm on the lower lumbar muscles just to one side of the spine. With the other hand, pull your partner's leg up. You can add a little rotation to the pulling to increase the effect.

6 Ya fa ▽   p 79

Use Ya fa (suppressing) with the tip of your elbow on Bl 36 and GB 30. Hold the suppression for 1 minute on each point on both sides.

7 Yi zhi chan tui fa   p 68

Use Yi zhi chan tui fa (one finger meditation) on Bl 40 for 3 minutes on each leg with the movement directed towards your partner's back.

8 Zhen fa   p 84

Use Zhen fa (vibrating), with the tip of your middle finger on GV 4 for 3 minutes.

9 Ji fa   p 82

Use Ji fa (chopping) on the lumbar muscles, all over the buttocks and down the backs of the legs for 3–4 minutes.

10 Ca fa   p 76

Use Ca fa (scrubbing) with a little dong qing gao ointment (see page 56) across the lumbar spine, using either the palm or the little-finger edge of your hand. Do this until the lower back feels scorching hot.

135

Sciatica

Sciatica is another very common musculoskeletal ailment that I treat frequently in my practice. In terms of causes, it can be grouped together with low back pain. It is most frequently related to an excess pattern, such as an invasion of wind damp cold.

Sciatica normally starts with lower back ache and, as the condition develops, pain is felt shooting down the buttock and the back or the lateral side of the leg, sometimes as far as the foot. The meridians affected are the bladder and gall bladder meridians. The pain of sciatica is usually only on one side. It is quite intense and is often described as feeling like an electric shock. At first it comes and goes but, if not treated in time, it can become constant.

As with other problems of the lower back, Tui Na treatment produces excellent results with sciatica. Often the radiating pain down the leg disappears after 2 or 3 treatments and the remaining low back pain is cleared up in a further 3–4 treatments. I recommend to my patients with sciatica and lower back ache that they come for maintenance and preventive treatments once every 3–4 weeks for 3 months after the problem has been alleviated.

Opposite is a simple Tui Na treatment that will help in all cases of sciatica to eliminate pathogenic factors that are obstructing the leg meridians and to encourage the flow of Qi and blood.

The exercises for low back pain *(see pages 133–4)* are equally important and effective in cases of sciatica. Gentle exercise such as walking will also help to keep Qi and blood moving through the meridians.

Treatment principle

Relax the tendons and muscles, invigorate the flow of Qi and blood, expel pathogenic factors and ease pain.

Course of treatment

1 treatment, 3 times per week for 3–4 weeks.

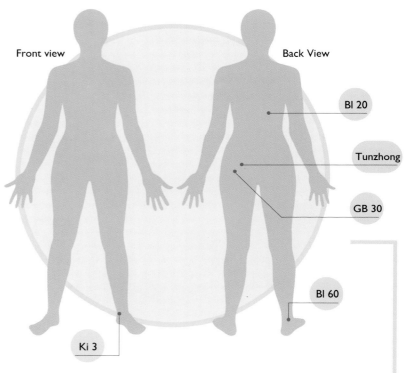

Front view

Back View

BI 20

Tunzhong

GB 30

BI 60

Ki 3

Quick point-finder for sciatica

You will find the points highlighted here used in the treatment of sciatica shown opposite. These diagrams are a quick reminder *(for exact point location see pages 48–53)*.

Treating sciatica

1 Gun fa   p 66

With your partner lying on their front, use Gun fa (rolling) on the affected side of the lumbar muscles, down over the buttock and the back and lateral side of the leg to the foot. Do this for 15 minutes, gradually building up the pace and pressure.

2 An fa   p 78

Use An fa (pressing) with the heels of both palms down the bladder meridian from the waist area all the way down the affected leg. Do this 3 times.

3 Ya fa   p 79

Use Ya fa (suppressing) on GB 30 and extra point Tunzhong on the affected side. Hold the suppression for 2–3 minutes on each point, gradually increasing the pressure.

4 Ji fa ▽   p 82

Apply Ji fa (dotting) on Bl 20, using your middle fingertip in much the same way as if you were using all your fingers. Work on both sides for 2–3 minutes.

5 An fa   p 78

Again working on Bl 20, apply pressing technique with your thumb. Stimulate the point on both sides for 3 minutes.

6 Na fa   p 74

Use Na fa (grasping) on Bl 60 and Ki 3 by firmly grasping both points either side of the Achilles tendon simultaneously. Do this for 2 minutes on the affected side.

7 Rou fa   p 70

Use Rou fa (kneading) with the heel of your palm on the gluteus muscles all around the GB 30 area on the affected side for about 5 minutes.

8 An rou fa   p 89

Use An rou fa (revolving) with your forearm on the lower lumbar muscles for 3–4 minutes, working briskly and strongly.

9 Ji fa   p 82

Use chopping technique with the little-finger edges of your palms and palms separated. Work up and down along the bladder meridian from the waist area to the foot of the affected side. Do this 3 times.

10 Ca fa ◁   p 76

Use Ca fa (scrubbing) with a little dong qing gao ointment (*see page 56*) across the lower lumbar area using the little-finger edge of your palm until the area is scorching hot.

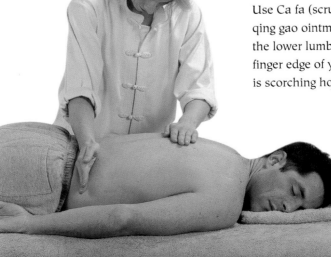

Conclusion

I hope that this book has served to provide you with a taste for Tui Na. You should now have an insight into the fascinating world of Chinese medicine and some practical hands-on tools that you can make use of in daily life to help your family and friends when they are unwell or in pain. Over the years that I have

been practising Tui Na I have realized that it is quite a wonderful thing to have at your fingertips a skill that can stop or ease someone's pain there and then without the use of medicines, drugs or invasive procedures. All that you need is your knowledge, your intuition and your hands. You could be anywhere in the world, in any situation – from a party to a train journey – and be able to do something to help.

My involvement in Chinese medicine has developed into a path of much personal growth, learning and discovery. Through practising Tui Na and Qi Gong, my own health, strength and vitality have greatly increased and I have found within myself a deep love and compassion for my fellow human beings. There are many rewards and benefits to be gained from practising Tui Na. It is a beautifully versatile healing art. One never gets bored – Tui Na keeps you on your toes and there is always room for improvement. My friend, teacher and the founder of the London School of Chinese Massage Therapy, Robert Cran, taught me that the Tui Na practitioner is an interesting and unusual breed by the fact that they must enjoy both mental stimulation and hands-on physical work.

For further information regarding training and for any enquiries connected to Tui Na, see Resources *(opposite)*.

Resources

If you are interested in training to become a Tui Na practitioner, there are full TCM Tui Na courses available in the USA, Australia and throughout the TCM colleges in China.

If you live in the UK, although there are a few short courses available teaching Tui Na techniques, there are at present no full three-year TCM practitioner's Tui Na courses running. However, myself and my colleagues at the Register of Chinese Massage Therapy hope to be offering some courses over the next few years with a view to recommencing the three-year diploma course of the London School of Chinese Massage Therapy. There is also a one-year course at the University of Westminster on Qi Gong Tui Na with Chinese Medicine Theory. For information on this contact the university at 115 New Cavendish Street, London W1M 8JS, Tel. (020) 7911 5000, Fax. (020) 7 911 5079, Email: armstron@wmin.ac.uk, Website: www.wmin.ac.uk.

For further information regarding training and for any enquiries connected to Tui Na, contact the organizations listed below, which have been set up to maintain the standards of Tui Na and to promote its practice.

Accreditation Commission for Acupuncture and Oriental Medicine (ACAOM) and Council of Colleges of Acupuncture and Oriental Medicine (CCAOM)
1010 Wayne Avenue, Suite 1270,
Silver Spring, MD 20910, USA
Tel: (301) 608 9680/9175   Fax: (301) 608 9576
Website: www.ccaom.org

Register of Chinese Massage Therapy
48 Lockhurst Street, London E5 0AP, UK

Australian Acupuncture Association Ltd
PO Box 5142, West End, Brisbane 4101, Australia
Tel: 07 3846 5866   Fax: 07 3846 5276
Email: aaca@eis.net.au

Further reading

The theory of traditional Chinese medicine

The Foundations of Chinese Medicine, Giovanni Maciocia. Edinburgh: Churchill Livingstone, 1989.

A Manual of Acupuncture, Deadman and Al-Khafaji. East Sussex: Journal of Chinese Medicine Publications, 1998.

The Practice of Chinese Medicine, Giovanni Maciocia. Edinburgh: Churchill Livingstone, 1994.

The Web that has No Weaver, Ted J. Kaptchuk. Chicago: Contemporary Books, 1997.

Zang Fu: the organ systems of traditional Chinese medicine, Jeremy Ross. Edinburgh: Churchill Livingstone, 1986.

Chinese massage

Chinese Massage, Wang Guocai, Fan Yali and Guan Zhang (Ed. Zhang Enqin). Shanghai: Publishing House of Shanghai College of Traditional Chinese Medicine, 1990.

Chinese Massage Therapy, (Ed.) Sun Chengman. Shangdon: Shangdon Science and Technology Press, 1990.

Chinese Massage Therapy: a handbook of therapeutic massage, (trans.) Hor Ming Lee and Gregory Whincup. London: Routledge and Kegan Paul, 1983.

Pointing Therapy: a Chinese traditional therapeutic skill, Jia Li Hui and Jia Zhao Xiang. Shangdon: Shandong Science and Technology Press, 1987.

Index

Acknowledgements

I would like to take this opportunity to thank the individuals who have advised, supported, inspired and encouraged me throughout the challenging process of writing this book.

To my friend and teacher, Robert Cran, without whom I would not be practising Tui Na today, thank you for teaching, guiding and inspiring me, for introducing me to Eddison Sadd who commissioned me to write this book and for acting as my consultant when I became overwhelmed with theoretical information. To Sally O'Donnell, a great big thank you for typing up page after page of hand-written text onto disk at short notice, having just given birth to her daughter Millie. Thank you to Dr Roy Cotton for his calm support and enthusiastic help and advice. Thank you to two of my oldest friends, Michael Matus and Alison Chadwick, for modelling for the photographs; their brightness and wit helped to make the photoshoot days great fun. Thanks to Sue, the photographer, for her patience, for being on the ball and for the excellent lunches she and René provided. Thanks to my mum for her constant support and encouragement over the phone and to my dad for all his support over the years. Thank you to my partner Deirdre Cartwright for all the practical and emotional support she gave, for the psychological tips that helped me to keep going, for the pink highlighter pen and for her love and belief in me. Thank you to Jacqui Hawkins for all the useful tips and informative conversations. To all my patients, a big thank you.

Finally, thank you to my editors and all the team at Eddison Sadd for their encouragement and guidance throughout the writing process and for all their hard work that went into putting the whole book together.

EDDISON·SADD EDITIONS

Commissioning Editor *Liz Wheeler*
Editor *Sophie Bevan*
Proofreader *Michele Turney*
Indexer *Dorothy Frame*

Art Director *Elaine Partington*
Senior Art Editors *Jamie Hanson and Carmel O'Neill*
Art Editor *Hayley Cove*
Photographer *Sue Atkinson*
Illustrations *Aziz Khan*
Calligraphy *Fook Fah Chong*
Models *Alison Chadwick, Shavella Loh, Alain Li Ko Lun, Michael Matus and Carmel O'Neill*

Production *Karyn Claridge and Charles James*

Eddison Sadd would like to thank Virgo Bodywork Tables, London (Tel. 020 8802 5008) for the loan of the massage tables used in photography. And thanks also to Julie Carpenter for permission to use the illustrations on pages 30 and 46. The image on page 13 is reproduced courtesy of Wellcome Institute Library, London.